The Year of the PRINCESS

Gordon Honeycombe

With photographs by Tim Graham

MICHAEL JOSEPH/RAINBIRD

First published in Great Britain by
Michael Joseph Ltd
44 Bedford Square, London WC1
in association with
The Rainbird Publishing Group Ltd
40 Park Street, London W1Y 4DE
who designed and produced the book
1982
© 1982 Honeycombe House

ISBN 0 7181 2146 5

Designer: Martin Bristow

Text filmset by SX Composing Ltd, Rayleigh, Essex, England
Colour originated by Bridge Graphics Ltd, Hull, England
Printed in The Netherlands by Royal Smeets Offset BV, Weert

HALF-TITLE: *An enamelled box commemorating the marriage
of the Prince and Princess of Wales on 29 July 1981*

FRONTISPIECE: *The Princess of Wales accompanied Prince Charles
to the 'Splendours of the Gonzaga' Exhibition which he opened
at the Victoria and Albert Museum in London on 4 November 1981.
She wore a hand-painted chiffon crinoline designed by Bellville Sassoon.*

Contents

Illustration Acknowledgments

Most of the photographs reproduced in this book were taken by Tim Graham of London.

The publishers would like to thank the following who have also supplied pictures for reproduction in this book:

Reproduced by gracious permission of Her Majesty the Queen: 59, 60, 63, 64–5
Mrs R.V.M. Andersen, New Malden: 92
Associated Newspapers p.l.c.: 77 (left)
Theo Bergstrøm: 117 (below)
The British Library, London: 56 (Photo: Rainbird)
Calman: 123 (above right)
Camera Press Ltd: 14 (above); Photos: Patrick Lichfield – 21 (above), 22, 23; Photo: Snowdon – 115
The Central Press Photos Ltd: 15, 18, 70, 98, 99 (right), 102, 113 (right)
The College of Arms, London: 25, 67
Colour Library International: 8
Daily Telegraph Colour Library: 26
Department of the Environment: 86
Eastern Daily Press, Norwich: 74
Mary Evans Picture Library: 61
Eugene Fleury: artwork for genealogical tables on 24–5, 66–7, and the map on 44
Fox Photos Ltd: 31, 132

Halcyon Days, London: half-title (Photo: Rainbird)
Alan Hamilton: 123 (above right)
Hamlyn Group Picture Library: 84 (top)
Peter Harding, Tetbury: 88, 127
Anwar Hussein: 100–1
Landywood Cabinet Co. Ltd: 89 (Photo: Acorn)
London Express News and Features Services: 30 (below), 122–3 (Drawing by Roy Castle)
Mansell Collection: 55, 57, 83
Jeremy Marks (Woodmansterne Ltd): 118
National Portrait Gallery, London: 54, 58, 62
Northampton Mercury Co. Ltd: 71
Photographers International: 37
The Press Association Ltd: 97 (top), 119, 122 (centre); Photos: Rainbird – 17, 69, 73
Rainbird Picture Library: 76, 77 (right)
Syndication International: 20, 43
Times Newspapers Ltd: 123 (above right)
Gerd Treuhaft: 10–11, 42, 99 (left)
Denis Waugh/Sunday Times: 12–13
Russell Whitehurst, Yass, Australia: 131
John Witherow: 123 (above right)

Illustrations for Chapter 12 on 'Birthday' were chosen after this page went to press but are acknowledged at the end of the book.

Author's Acknowledgments

My thanks to all those authors, writers, commentators, reporters and journalists who have already written exhaustively and for the most part truthfully about the Princess of Wales. My particular thanks to those friends and relatives of the Prince and Princess who helped with pictures and in correcting facts; to Michael Shea and the Press Office at Buckingham Palace for much invaluable assistance; to the Daily Telegraph Information Service; to BBC Television and ITN; and to those friends, advisers, PR ladies, press officers and experts, without whose specialized aid and knowledge this book could not have been written – especially Mrs Angus Blair, Brenda Birmingham, Isobel Davie, Suzy Menkes, Jean Rook, Jenny Turton, Michael Andrews, Peter Godfrey, and Edward Rayne. My thanks above all to Nicholas Courtney, Bryan Rostron and Tim Graham, and (at Rainbird) to Georgina Evans, David Roberts and Michael O'Mara.

Books and magazines that were particularly helpful in my research were: *Prince Charles, Monarch in the Making*, by Douglas Liversidge, published by Arthur Barker, 1975; *Britain's Royal Brides*, by Josy Argy and Wendy Riches, published by David and Charles, 1975; *Majesty*, by Robert Lacey, published by Hutchinson, 1977; *Charles, Prince of Wales*, by Anthony Holden, published by Weidenfeld & Nicolson, 1979; *Royal Palaces, Castles & Homes*, by Patrick Montague-Smith and Hugh Montgomery-Massingberd, published by Country Life Books, 1981; *The Queen & Her Court*, by Jerrold M. Packard, published by Robson Books, 1981; *Royal Wedding*, by Gordon Honeycombe, published by Michael Joseph and Rainbird, 1981; *Diana, Princess of Wales*, by Nicholas Courtney, published by Park Lane Press, 1982; *Edward III*, by Paul Johnson, published by Weidenfeld & Nicolson, 1973; *Richard III*, by Anthony Cheetham, published by Weidenfeld & Nicolson, 1972; *Catherine the Queen*, by Mary M. Lukes, published by Frederick Muller, 1968; *George IV, Regent and King*, by Christopher Hibbert, published by Allen Lane, 1973; *Edward VII*, by Christopher Hibbert, published by Allen Lane, 1976; and the magazines *Majesty* and *Royalty*.

G.H., London, 1982.

CHAPTER ONE

Marriage

'FORASMUCH AS CHARLES PHILIP ARTHUR GEORGE and Diana Frances have consented together in holy wedlock, and have witnessed the same before God and this company, and thereto have given and pledged their troth either to other, and have declared the same by giving and receiving of a ring, and by joining of hands; I pronounce that they be man and wife together, in the name of the Father, and of the Son, and of the Holy Ghost. Amen.'

So said the Archbishop of Canterbury, and so began the first royal year of the ninth Princess of Wales.

Engaged six months earlier, when she was nineteen and a half, the former nursery assistant, albeit the daughter of an earl, became the wife of the heir to the throne of England, Scotland, Wales and Northern Ireland and future head of the Commonwealth. Before the eyes of the world, of the biggest television audience in history, she formally exchanged the sheltered anonymity of an aristocratic background for a very public but protected life, blessed with extraordinary privilege and wealth and dedicated to old-fashioned but not outmoded ideals of service, duty and the perpetuation of that most ancient of institutions, monarchy. Her children would be princes of the realm. She herself, already known all over the world, would one day become the richest woman in the kingdom and its Queen.

Her first royal year began just after 11.15 on the morning of Wednesday, 29 July 1981, in St Paul's Cathedral, London, when the Lady Diana Spencer, a month after her twentieth birthday, became the Princess of Wales.

Her last day as a private citizen, a commoner, had begun in the regal surroundings of Clarence House, the London home of the bridegroom's grandmother, Queen Elizabeth the Queen Mother. Here she had also spent the first night of her engagement. The evening before

---

On 28 July 1981, the night before the wedding, a spectacular firework display, set against a specially built palace façade, was staged in Hyde Park in aid of the International Year of the Disabled.

her wedding, like millions of others, she had watched television after dinner and had seen her fiancé, Prince Charles, light a beacon in Hyde Park, the first in a chain of 101 bonfires and beacons that would be lit nationwide that night. A spectacular but disorganized firework display followed, intermixed with gun salvoes, music from massed bands and choirs, all watched by a huge crowd of half a million. Such a firework display had not been seen in Britain for more than two hundred years. She had seen her fiancé's family arrive and depart in stately limousines through avenues of torchlight, while many distinguished and royal wedding guests were transported to and from Buckingham Palace in a fleet of less-than-stately hired coaches. The next time she would see him, his family and their 2,500 guests would be at eleven o'clock the following morning, when she in turn would be the cynosure of all eyes in the Cathedral and around the world.

The next day she woke early in Clarence House with scarcely any appetite and an anxious eye on the weather. But the day was calm and bright: the sun shone through a golden haze. Assisted by her hairdresser, make-up lady, dressmakers and maids, she began to prepare herself for her wedding, arraying herself in the dress that had excited so much female speculation and would soon be publicly displayed for the first time and described by the media. The Queen Mother paid her a visit. So did her grandmother, Lady Fermoy. The rest of her family, all looking their best, dropped in to embrace her and wish her well before departing at scheduled times to take their seats in the Cathedral.

At 10.10 her mother, Frances Shand Kydd, left Clarence House by car with her second husband, Peter, and her seventeen-year-old son, Charles, Viscount Althorp. Ten minutes later the bridesmaids and pageboys set out for the Cathedral from Clarence House, and at 10.22 the Queen's Carriage procession of eight landaus left Buckingham Palace, followed at 10.30 by the two-carriage procession of the Prince of Wales. Perhaps the bride glimpsed some of this on television, as she waited with her father, Earl Spencer, for her own departure, timed for 10.35. More probably, she was concerned about last-minute adjustments to her dress and appearance: the attaching of the 25-foot-long train to her waist; the donning of the wide, tulle veil and the Spencer family tiara – which was the 'something old' she wore that day. As 'something blue' she wore a specially-made blue garter, and the 'something borrowed' for good luck was a pair of her mother's diamond earrings.

Then it was time to pack herself, her dress, her veil, and voluminous train into the cramped interior of the Glass Coach with her father. The Queen Mother's household gathered on the steps of Clarence House to wave and applaud, relishing the last privileged private view they had of the bride before she was seen by the world. With a little lurch and two minutes late, the immaculate coach, drawn by a pair of bay horses, moved out of the gates of Clarence House into Stable Yard Road and thence into The Mall and the enveloping cheers of the crowds who had stood waiting for hours.

For twenty minutes she was borne through the sunny streets of London on a dazzling sea of cheering faces, waving hands, clicking cameras, red, white and blue banners and flags. Lines of servicemen facing her presented arms, while policemen, their backs to her, watched the crowds. She smiled and waved at the myriad of people. She seemed enraptured. The day itself, her wedding day, was special enough without all this. But for the time being, cocooned as she was in the Glass Coach, the view through her veil and the coach's three glass panels must have made the passing spectacle seem like a moving triptych, partly blocked by the back of a black-uniformed police sergeant on a large bay horse. As she was still a commoner, her escort was not a royal one: it was composed of mounted civil and military police. 'It's wonderful to see people's enthusiastic reaction,' she said later. 'A mass of smiling faces. It's most rewarding and gives me a tremendous boost.'

From The Mall, the coach progressed along the Strand, Fleet Street and up Ludgate Hill to St Paul's Cathedral, swinging left around the statue of Queen Anne, which was shielded by boards and further obscured by a mass of photographers and television cameras. The coach slowed and swung to a halt below the steps of St Paul's.

The door was opened by a footman clad in the scarlet and gold State Livery. Her father, who had still not fully recovered from a stroke some years ago, descended first, helped by his chauffeur, John. She

Lady Diana Spencer travelled in the Glass Coach from Clarence House to St Paul's Cathedral with her father, Earl Spencer, escorted by the Royal Military Police and Metropolitan Police. The coach, built in 1910, was bought by George V for his coronation in June 1911.

followed, gathering up the taffeta folds of her dress, careful to keep the skirt off the sanded road and to step onto the red carpet which stretched before her up twenty-four wide steps to the great West Door.

The Crown Equerry, Lieutenant-Colonel Sir John Miller, and two of her bridesmaids, Lady Sarah Armstrong-Jones and India Hicks, greeted her, the girls ready to take charge of her train, catching and spreading it as it flowed out of the coach behind her. With apparent confidence she ascended the steps, which were lined by officers of the three services. Her father accompanied her, still supported by his chauffeur dressed in a morning coat. A fanfare, played by the State Trumpeters, resounded from the portico above her, brassily ringing out over the cheering crowds. Suddenly she was inside the comparative gloom of the vast, glittering Cathedral.

Here she was greeted by the Dean of St Paul's, by the Bishop of London and the Archbishop of Canterbury, the latter wearing a gleaming new blue and silver cope. Then the bridal procession formed. Her dressmakers and bridesmaids fussed around her dress and veil as, outside, the Cathedral clock struck eleven. With Earl Spencer stoutly clasping her left arm in his crooked right arm, preceded by eleven senior members of the clergy garbed in red, silver and gold and followed by her seven bridesmaids and page-boys, she began the long three-and-a-half-minute walk up the red-carpeted nave, while a Trumpet Voluntary was played by the organ and orchestra. 'I was so nervous,' she said later. 'I hardly knew what I was doing.'

Her father took the centre of the aisle, as if to steady his direction, and she found herself walking near the congregation on her right, her train swishing past their chairs. Through her veil she saw people's heads and faces turn towards her and smile, the women's colourful hats and costumes making a most fashionable show. She looked for friends, smiling at people she knew: her own friends were on the other, left-hand side of the aisle. It was not until the clergy moved apart that she saw her future husband, dressed as a Commander in the Royal Navy – in the Navy's No. 1 ceremonial dress uniform and wearing a blue Garter sash. Standing with his younger brothers, Prince Andrew and Prince Edward, who would act as 'supporters' – there was no best man – he was looking back down the aisle towards

The bride ascends the steps of St Paul's with her father, and her bridesmaids, Lady Sarah Armstrong-Jones and India Hicks, adjust her train. The guard of honour, facing the Cathedral, was mounted by the Royal Navy, the 1st Battalion of the Royal Regiment of Wales, and the Royal Air Force, Brawdy. Behind, stands the Band of the Royal Marines. The officers lining the steps were friends of the Prince from the three services.

ABOVE: *As the bride moved up the aisle of the Cathedral she was followed by her five bridesmaids and two page-boys, all children of the bridegroom's relatives and friends: (left to right) Lady Sarah Armstrong-Jones, Lord Nicholas Windsor, India Hicks, Edward van Cutsem, Sarah Jane Gaselee, Catherine Cameron, and Clementine Hambro.*

RIGHT: *During the bride's procession the organ and orchestra played the 'Trumpet Voluntary' by Jeremiah Clarke. 'I want everyone to come out having had a marvellous musical and emotional experience,' said the Prince beforehand. And so they did.*

her. He smiled at her and moved forward as she approached him. 'You look wonderful,' he whispered. 'Wonderful for you,' she replied.

Then they were standing side by side on the dais before the choir and the high altar. Her chief bridesmaid, Lady Sarah, took her bouquet from her. Glancing cautiously about, she caught the welcoming smiles of the bridegroom's family on her right and of her own family to the left of the dais. The Prince, relinquishing his grip on the hilt of his sword, grasped the fingers of her right hand – her left continued to act as a steadying prop for her father's arm. Prince Andrew passed a large white programme containing the Order of Service to

The Archbishop of Canterbury pronounced the couple man and wife and offered his blessing. Earlier his Address began, 'This is the stuff of which fairy tales are made . . .' In the background are the Queen, Prince Philip and the Queen Mother.

the bridegroom and the marriage ceremony, without further preamble, began with a hymn.

The young bride stood between her future husband and her father, abstractedly aware of them, of the enveloping mist of her veil, of the silken weight of her dress, the red lamps of the choir-stalls, and the majestic sounds of choir and congregation singing the hymn 'Christ is made the sure foundation'. It ended. Then she heard the Dean of St Paul's begin to speak the familiar and now irrevocable words of the Solemnization of Matrimony, rehearsed two days before.

'Dearly beloved, we are gathered here in the sight of God and in the face of this congregation to join together this man and this woman . . .' As he finished speaking, there was the inevitable moment of mild suspense when he asked, 'If any man can show any just cause why they may not lawfully be joined together, let him now speak, or else hereafter for ever hold his peace.'

Prince Philip turned his head to look at the congregation, but no voice was heard, and the Archbishop of Canterbury moved in front of Lady Diana and the Prince of Wales to make his charge and take them through their vows.

Prince Charles reassuringly squeezed her fingers, his intertwined with hers, smiling sideways at her more than once. Then she looked at him, listening as he solemnly regarded the Archbishop and with some feeling made the first of his vows, 'I will.'

The Archbishop turned to her. She heard him ask her, 'Wilt thou love him, comfort him, honour and keep him, in sickness and in health; and forsaking all other, keep thee only unto him, so long as ye both shall live?'

It was her turn to speak. As firmly as she might, she replied, 'I will.'

'Who giveth this woman to be married to this man?'

Her father now unloosed his hold on her, leading her left hand forward, which the Archbishop took, guiding it into the Prince's right hand. Now he plighted his troth, concentrating on repeating the Archbishop's words. 'I, Charles Philip Arthur George . . .'

With downcast eyes she heard the finality of this vow – 'To have and to hold from this day forward, for better for worse, for richer for poorer, in sickness and in health, to love and to cherish, till death us do part' – and possibly she heard the faint cheers of the crowds outside who listened as the service was relayed to them.

Perhaps something flustered her as the Archbishop made them release their hands before prompting her to take the Prince's right hand, this time in hers. Perhaps her realization of the full import of the occasion and what she was about to say unnerved her – she always rushed her words when she was nervous, and now she had to say more than she had ever said in public before, and make her vows.

'I Diana Frances,' she began, speaking after the Archbishop, 'take thee Philip Charles Arthur George . . .'

Shamed and confused at having mixed up his names, she seemed about to stop. Behind her veil she blushed. But the Archbishop continued speaking, and so did she. The Prince beside her grinned, realizing she had erred, and tightened his grasp of her hand. However, she made no more mistakes and at the end of her vows the Archbishop whispered, 'Well done.'

The service continued with the blessing of the ring, which Prince Andrew passed to Prince Charles who put it on the fourth finger of her left hand, looking earnestly at her and saying, 'With this ring I thee wed; with my body I thee honour . . .' Then he erred, as if in sympathy, omitting a word and altering another. He said, 'All thy goods with thee I share', instead of, 'All my worldly goods . . .' No doubt she felt better after that.

But now she had time to recover: they knelt before the Archbishop while he offered a prayer for them both. In a moment he joined their hands together for the last time, saying, 'Those whom God hath joined together let no man put asunder.' He then pronounced them man and wife.

They now seemed much more relaxed. As they seated themselves on stools, Viscount Althorp assisted his father to a seat. The choirs then sang William Mathias's new anthem set to the words of Psalm 67, 'Let the people praise thee, O God' – during which the choirmaster, energetically conducting, knocked a red lamp off the light nearest him. Even the Queen, who had hidden her emotions behind an almost expressionless mask, smiled and was amused by the incident.

There was now an air of celebration, and the service proceeded with the Lesson from I Corinthians 13, read by the Speaker of the House of Commons, the Right Honourable George Thomas, and the Address, given by Doctor Runcie, the Archbishop of Canterbury.

As another anthem – 'I was glad' by Hubert Parry – was sung, the Prince and Princess moved up the choir to the high altar, conversing easily as the splendid music of the anthem soared above them. They and the congregation then knelt for prayers, responses and further prayers by three leading representatives of the Church of England, the Roman Catholic Church and the Church of Scotland, and by the Reverend Harry Williams, formerly Dean of Prince Charles's College in Cambridge, who was the first to refer to the bride as 'Diana, Princess of Wales'.

After the Lord's Prayer, a hymn chosen by the bride was sung – 'I vow to thee my country' – before the final blessing, the sung 'Amen' and a superb new arrangement of the National Anthem by Sir David Willcocks, Director of the Royal College of Music.

The Prince and Princess then left the nave, she still attended by Lady Sarah Armstrong-Jones. They were led by the Archbishop into the south aisle and followed by the Dean and Chapter of St Paul's, by the Queen, Prince Philip, their daughter and their two other sons; by Earl Spencer, Mrs Shand Kydd and Lady Fermoy. Two registers were signed, the State one and a royal register which is kept in the Lord Chamberlain's Office and commemorates over one hundred years of royal weddings and christenings. While this was happening, 'Let the bright seraphim', an aria and

BELOW: The Prince and Princess of Wales paused as they emerged into the sunshine and acknowledged the cheering crowds.

LEFT: After the registers had been signed, the orchestra played Elgar's 'Pomp and Circumstance March No. 4 in G' and Walton's 'Crown Imperial' as the bride and groom walked down the aisle towards the West Door of the Cathedral.

chorus from Handel's oratorio *Samson*, was sung by the New Zealand soprano, Miss Kiri Te Kanawa, and the Bach Choir. Princess Margaret did not sign the registers – for the simple reason that an aunt seldom does so. She and her son, Viscount Linley, remained in their seats.

A triumphant fanfare, played by the State Trumpeters in the Whispering Gallery below the Great Dome, announced the return of the bride and groom, the bride with her veil raised. Now she saw everyone perfectly, and all could see her face. Once again carrying her bouquet, and happily talking to the Prince, she advanced with him down the choir. Just as they reached the dais where they had made their vows, the full orchestra, conducted by Sir Colin Davis, began playing the noble music of 'Pomp and Circumstance March No. 4 in G' by Elgar. The Princess turned towards the Queen and curtseyed low as the Prince bowed. They then walked out into the congregation, the Princess looking to her right where her friends and relatives stood, and returned their smiles.

They emerged from the West Door at ten past twelve as a peal of twelve bells from the northwest tower of St Paul's was answered by others singing out

RIGHT: *The Prince and Princess travelled to Buckingham Palace in the State Postillion Landau which was built in 1902 for Edward VII. It was drawn by four grey Postillion horses and contained a silver horseshoe for luck.*
BELOW: *The families of the bride and groom watched from the West Door as the royal couple left St Paul's Cathedral. Mrs Shand Kydd, the bride's mother, is seen (left) standing with the Queen and Earl Spencer.*

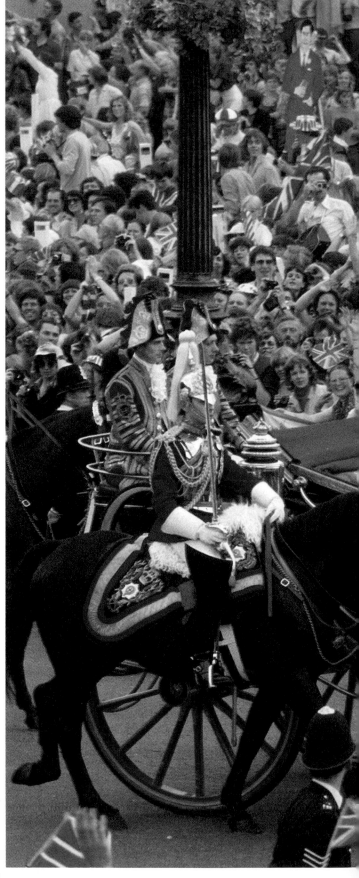

LEFT: *At the Grand Entrance in the inner quadrangle of Buckingham Palace the royal couple paused to smile for photographers.*
BELOW: *The huge crowds outside the Palace were rewarded by five balcony appearances before the guests sat down for the wedding breakfast at 2.30 p.m.*

ABOVE: *In the Picture Gallery of Buckingham Palace, the Princess talks to her youngest bridesmaid, five-year-old Clementine Hambro, while the Queen looks on. The Princess still carries her bouquet of gardenias, roses, orchids, stephanotis, lilies of the valley, freesias, myrtle and veronica.*

in the City. The crowd roared. 'Give them a wave,' the Prince suggested, and the Princess obliged with her first rather modest royal wave.

Other 'firsts' followed: when the Queen allowed Earl Spencer to precede her into the Semi-State Postillion landau before her procession returned to Buckingham Palace through the joyful crowds; when the bridal couple, their parents and other members of the royal family, appeared on the balcony at Buckingham Palace for the first time at ten-past one and the bridegroom kissed the hand of the bride; and when, ten minutes later, at their fourth appearance, the Prince, encouraged by Prince Andrew, kissed his bride on the lips.

Such a public demonstration of royal affection had never been seen by so many, nor had so many hundreds of thousands ever sung such a heart-felt chorus of 'You'll never walk alone' – usually reserved for football heroes. 'We want Charlie!' 'We want Di!' the crowds

ABOVE AND LEFT: *The official wedding photographs were taken in the Throne Room at Buckingham Palace, by Lord Lichfield, a cousin of the Queen.*

chanted, calling next for the Queen Mother and the Queen. They were rewarded by a fifth balcony appearance at twenty-past two, after the official wedding photographs had been taken in the Throne Room by Lord Lichfield. These also displayed more than one rare picture of royal informality, as well as an unusual domestic touch: a white background was provided for some pictures by a royal bedsheet.

The wedding breakfast, preceded by a reception in the Picture Gallery, was held in the Ball Supper Room and began at about half past two. The three-course luncheon, including *Suprême de volaille Princesse de Galles*, was attended by 118 people: close relatives of the Prince and Princess being outnumbered by the Queen's royal and State guests. They were democratically served at twelve round tables. In another break with tradition, the wedding cake, hexagonal and five-tiered, was not made by royal caterers but by the Royal Navy's Cookery School at Chatham. It was cut by the Prince and Princess, using his ceremonial sword, after the Prince had replied to the toast to the bride and

groom, proposed jointly by his two younger brothers. For the first time on such an occasion, no other toasts were proposed.

The usual rose petals and confetti were thrown by guests and members of the royal household as the bridal couple left the inner quadrangle of the Palace at 4.20 p.m. But exceptional were the blue and silver balloons attached to their carriage and the banner behind it bearing the proclamation 'Just Married'. The bride herself broke with tradition by not wearing white gloves with her short-sleeved dress. Security, at its greatest ever on a royal occasion, demanded that one of the footmen perched behind the happy pair be in reality an armed policeman – a matter that discomfited the Princess when it came to her attention.

They drove to Waterloo Station, where at Platform 12 they boarded a special train for Romsey in Hampshire. It set off on its eighty-mile journey at 4.40 p.m., ten minutes late. Its engine, called *Broadlands*, bore the same name as the home of Lord and Lady Romsey, formerly Earl Mountbatten's home, where shortly after 6 p.m. the honeymoon couple arrived.

The eighteenth-century country house had been closed to the public since Monday and temporarily vacated by Lord Romsey, a good friend and cousin of

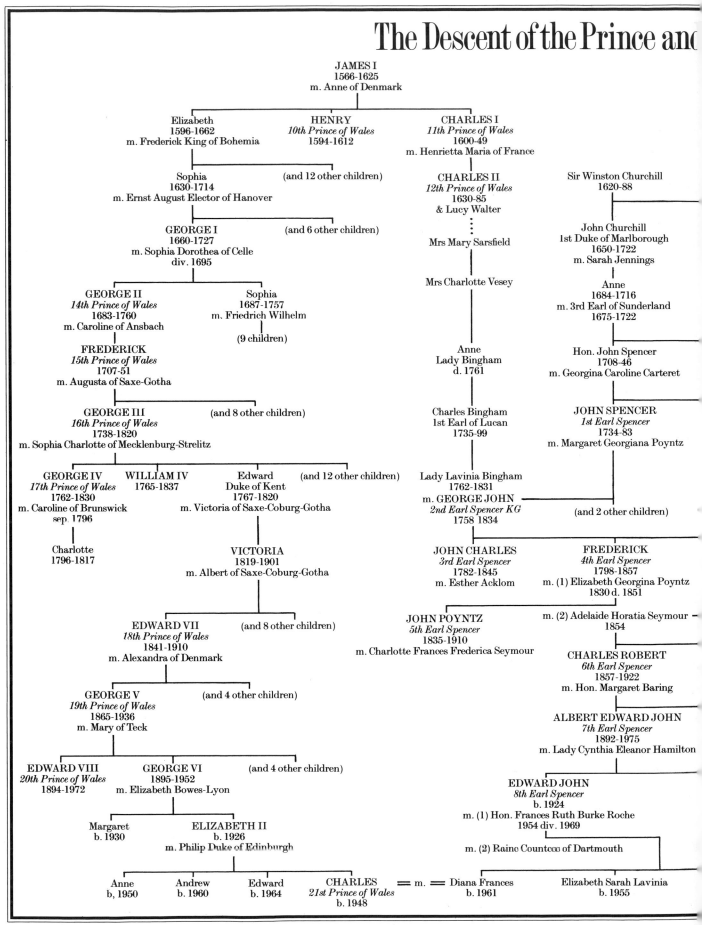

JAMES I
1566-1625
m. Anne of Denmark

Elizabeth
1596-1662
m. Frederick King of Bohemia

HENRY
10th Prince of Wales
1594-1612

CHARLES I
11th Prince of Wales
1600-49
m. Henrietta Maria of France

Sophia
1630-1714
m. Ernst August Elector of Hanover

(and 12 other children)

CHARLES II
12th Prince of Wales
1630-85
& Lucy Walter

Sir Winston Churchill
1620-88

GEORGE I
1660-1727
m. Sophia Dorothea of Celle
div. 1695

(and 6 other children)

Mrs Mary Sarsfield

John Churchill
1st Duke of Marlborough
1650-1722
m. Sarah Jennings

GEORGE II
14th Prince of Wales
1683-1760
m. Caroline of Ansbach

Sophia
1687-1757
m. Friedrich Wilhelm

(9 children)

Mrs Charlotte Vesey

Anne
1684-1716
m. 3rd Earl of Sunderland
1675-1722

FREDERICK
15th Prince of Wales
1707-51
m. Augusta of Saxe-Gotha

Anne
Lady Bingham
d. 1761

Hon. John Spencer
1708-46
m. Georgina Caroline Carteret

GEORGE III
16th Prince of Wales
1738-1820
m. Sophia Charlotte of Mecklenburg-Strelitz

(and 8 other children)

Charles Bingham
1st Earl of Lucan
1735-99

JOHN SPENCER
1st Earl Spencer
1734-83
m. Margaret Georgiana Poyntz

GEORGE IV
17th Prince of Wales
1762-1830
m. Caroline of Brunswick
sep. 1796

WILLIAM IV
1765-1837

Edward
Duke of Kent
1767-1820
m. Victoria of Saxe-Coburg-Gotha

(and 12 other children)

Lady Lavinia Bingham
1762-1831
m. GEORGE JOHN
2nd Earl Spencer KG
1758-1834

(and 2 other children)

Charlotte
1796-1817

VICTORIA
1819-1901
m. Albert of Saxe-Coburg-Gotha

JOHN CHARLES
3rd Earl Spencer
1782-1845
m. Esther Acklom

FREDERICK
4th Earl Spencer
1798-1857
m. (1) Elizabeth Georgina Poyntz
1830 d. 1851

EDWARD VII
18th Prince of Wales
1841-1910
m. Alexandra of Denmark

(and 8 other children)

JOHN POYNTZ
5th Earl Spencer
1835-1910
m. Charlotte Frances Frederica Seymour

m. (2) Adelaide Horatia Seymour
1854

CHARLES ROBERT
6th Earl Spencer
1857-1922
m. Hon. Margaret Baring

GEORGE V
19th Prince of Wales
1865-1936
m. Mary of Teck

(and 4 other children)

ALBERT EDWARD JOHN
7th Earl Spencer
1892-1975
m. Lady Cynthia Eleanor Hamilton

EDWARD VIII
20th Prince of Wales
1894-1972

GEORGE VI
1895-1952
m. Elizabeth Bowes-Lyon

(and 4 other children)

EDWARD JOHN
8th Earl Spencer
b. 1924
m. (1) Hon. Frances Ruth Burke Roche
1954 div. 1969

Margaret
b. 1930

ELIZABETH II
b. 1926
m. Philip Duke of Edinburgh

m. (2) Raine Countess of Dartmouth

Anne
b. 1950

Andrew
b. 1960

Edward
b. 1964

CHARLES
21st Prince of Wales
b. 1948

═ m. ═ Diana Frances
b. 1961

Elizabeth Sarah Lavinia
b. 1955

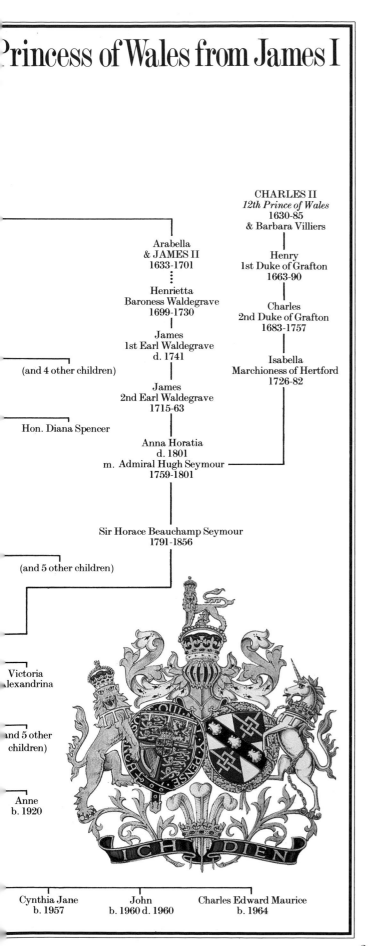

CHARLES II
12th Prince of Wales
1630-85
& Barbara Villiers

Arabella
& JAMES II
1633-1701

Henry
1st Duke of Grafton
1663-90

Henrietta
Baroness Waldegrave
1699-1730

Charles
2nd Duke of Grafton
1683-1757

James
1st Earl Waldegrave
d. 1741

(and 4 other children)

Isabella
Marchioness of Hertford
1726-82

James
2nd Earl Waldegrave
1715-63

Hon. Diana Spencer

Anna Horatia
d. 1801
m. Admiral Hugh Seymour
1759-1801

Sir Horace Beauchamp Seymour
1791-1856

(and 5 other children)

Victoria
Alexandrina

and 5 other
children)

Anne
b. 1920

Cynthia Jane
b. 1957

John
b. 1960 d. 1960

Charles Edward Maurice
b. 1964

the Prince who had been best man at his wedding to Penelope Eastwood. It was here at Broadlands that the Princess and her Prince would spend the first three nights of their married life, getting to know each other, and recovering, in the nearest royal equivalent of solitude, from what had been a highly enjoyable, exciting, exhausting and remarkable day.

Later that year, at London's Guildhall, on 5 November, the Prince said, 'We still think about it; we still can't quite get over what happened that day. Neither of us will ever forget the atmosphere. It was electric, I felt, and I know my wife agrees. The noise outside my bedroom window [in Buckingham Palace] was almost unbelievable, and I remember standing at my window trying to realize what it was like, so that I might tell my own children – which I shall now be able to do. It was something quite extraordinary . . . I was quite extraordinarily proud to be British.'

CHAPTER TWO

Honeymoon

T HE QUEEN AND PRINCE PHILIP also began their honeymoon at Broadlands, on 20 November 1947, before going on to Birkhall. By tradition, honeymoon couples at Broadlands occupy the Portico Room and the Green Room. These same rooms, overlooking the grounds and the River Test, were occupied by the Queen's eldest son and his bride on their wedding night, which was partly spent in reading how the evening newspapers had described the day's events and, after a light supper, watching edited versions of their wedding on television.

LEFT: *The bride and groom left Buckingham Palace for their honeymoon escorted by a Travelling Escort of the Household Cavalry. The Princess wore a coral-pink dress and jacket of silk tussore designed by Bellville Sassoon and a matching straw tricorn hat trimmed with ostrich feathers by John Boyd. The footman behind the Prince was a police officer.*

BELOW: *The royal couple began their honeymoon at Broadlands, an imposing Palladian mansion near Romsey and the former home of Prince Charles's great-uncle, the late Earl Mountbatten of Burma.*

Security was strict around the 6,000-acre estate: aircraft was prohibited from flying lower than 3,000 feet; a watch was kept on the river and the grounds were patrolled. As the staff at Broadlands also kept their peace, little is known about the couple's activities over the following two days except that they went for walks, that the Prince did some early evening fishing in the river (and caught nothing) and that the Princess went for a swim in the heated outdoor pool. Thursday was a fine summer's day; but on Friday evening there was thunder, lightning and rain.

The morning of Saturday, 1 August, was cool and damp. At 9.50 the honeymoon couple were driven the eight miles from Broadlands to Eastleigh Airport near Southampton. Delayed by crowds along the route, they arrived twenty minutes late and with little ceremony boarded an antiquated, twin-propellered Andover of the Queen's Flight. Take-off was at 10.25 and Prince Charles himself took the controls for the five-and-a-half-hour flight to Gibraltar. The Andover stopped at Oporto in Portugal to refuel, and, still piloted by the Prince (who only left the flight deck for a snack lunch) arrived at Gibraltar Airport, not far from the Spanish border, at 5 p.m. local time.

This private and informal stopover on a piece of British territory which Spain would like to reclaim, had caused the King and Queen of Spain to cancel their attendance at the wedding. As if to counteract such nationalism and display a different sort, the sunny, narrow streets of Gibraltar were a patriotic riot of red, white and blue, and thronged with joyously cheering, flag-waving British holidaymakers and Gibraltarians. Their enthusiasm clearly added to the royal couple's happy anticipation of their Mediterranean cruise, and their half-hour drive in an open-top brown Triumph Stag from the airport to the dockyard, turned into a carnival procession.

After boarding the Royal Yacht, *Britannia* – when the Prince's personal standard was broken at the mainmast and a 21-gun salute thundered from the naval shore-base, HMS *Rooke* – the Prince and Princess entertained the Governor of the colony, Sir William Jackson, his wife and some local dignitaries to drinks at six o'clock. One of the visitors, Lady Hassan, wife of Sir Joshua Hassan, Gibraltar's Chief Minister, said later, 'It was wonderful . . . They stood hand in hand while we chatted and kept looking into each other's eyes. It was beautiful to see two young people so devoted. The Princess was very moved by the welcome here. She kept peering out of the porthole and tears welled in her eyes. She was overwhelmed by it all.'

On the sun deck of the Royal Yacht, Prince Charles and his young wife held hands as Britannia *sailed from Gibraltar at the start of the honeymoon cruise.*

When the visitors left, the couple went out onto the sun deck at the stern of the ship and waved and watched as *Britannia* weighed anchor at 6.45 p.m. and put to sea. The Band of the First Staffords on the quay played 'Sailing', church bells rang, and crowds lining the shore and the south mole shouted and cheered. It was a romantic, emotional scene. On the sun deck the Princess was again observed to brush tears from her eyes. Slowly the Royal Yacht slid out into Algeciras Bay and into the golden blaze of the setting sun, before heading south and east around the massive white Rock of Gibraltar. The couple held hands, gazing about them at the brilliant sea, at the aquatic display put on by harbour craft, at the ragged flotilla of noisy, overcrowded yachts, motor cruisers and small boats that pursued them for a while, finally falling away, as *Britannia* forged ahead into the Mediterranean and vanished into the night.

The Royal Yacht had been utilized before as a honeymoon hotel – by Princess Margaret and Antony Armstrong-Jones when they toured the islands of the Caribbean in May 1960; and by Princess Anne and Captain Mark Phillips in November 1973 on another Caribbean cruise.

In 1953, Her Majesty's Yacht, *Britannia*, had replaced Queen Victoria's fifty-year-old yacht, *Victoria and Albert*, which had continued in royal service until World War II. The construction of a successor, mooted by Edward VIII, had been promulgated by George VI in 1951. HMY *Britannia*, built in John Brown's shipyards on Clydebank, was launched by the Queen in April 1953, less than two months before the Coronation. She said at the time, 'My father felt very strongly, as I do, that a yacht was a necessity, not a luxury, for the head of our great British Commonwealth, between whose countries the sea is no barrier, but the natural and indestructible highway.'

The Royal Yacht *Britannia* is rather unsteady, and the Queen, who is a poor sailor, would sometimes prefer

ABOVE: *The people of Gibraltar patriotically decorated their streets in red, white and blue to welcome the royal couple on the afternoon of Saturday, 1 August 1981.*
BELOW: *Her Majesty's Yacht* Britannia.

not to sail aboard the yacht at all. For, despite stabilizers, the ship has a tendency to rock and roll, especially in bad weather.

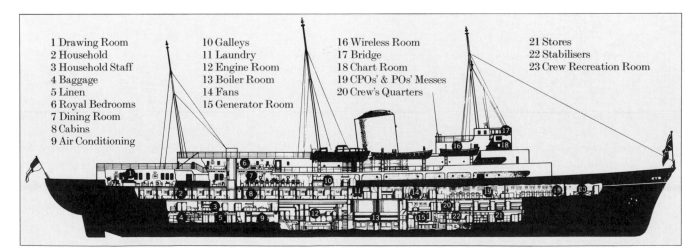

1 Drawing Room
2 Household
3 Household Staff
4 Baggage
5 Linen
6 Royal Bedrooms
7 Dining Room
8 Cabins
9 Air Conditioning
10 Galleys
11 Laundry
12 Engine Room
13 Boiler Room
14 Fans
15 Generator Room
16 Wireless Room
17 Bridge
18 Chart Room
19 CPOs' & POs' Messes
20 Crew's Quarters
21 Stores
22 Stabilisers
23 Crew Recreation Room

The royal apartments on Britannia *are aft on the weather decks. The spacious drawing-room is approached through an ante-room.*

Britannia is also expensive. More like a small liner than the common conception of a yacht, she is almost half as long as the QE2 and is maintained by the Ministry of Defence at an annual cost of about £2 million. She has had nine refits, the last major refit costing £5 million. The weekly wage bill of her crew of 277 is some £33,000. To pay her way and to offset the infrequent royal use that is made of her – she sails on royal business for only about four months each year – the 5,769-ton Royal Yacht (which could be used as a hospital ship in time of war) is employed on NATO and naval exercises, sometimes as a command headquarters or as a surrogate merchant ship in a convoy tracked by hypothetical enemy submarines. Her hull is painted dark blue, not black as it seems from a distance, and the upper deck is marked by a single gold band. *Britannia* bears no name – just the royal crest and cypher at her bow and stern respectively.

Her chief officer (since February 1981) is the Flag Officer, Royal Yachts, Rear-Admiral Paul Greening.

His Executive Officer, the man who steered the ship on the honeymoon cruise, was Commander Michael Moore. Despite Rear-Admiral Greening's title there is only *one* royal yacht. The yachts and boats used for sailing by the royal family are privately owned.

Britannia has twenty-one officers in all. They serve on board her for two years, as do half of the 256 other ranks; the rest of them form a permanent crew, staying with the ship throughout their years with the Royal Navy. Handpicked volunteers, they are called 'Yachtsmen'. However, they are paid no special rate and receive no special allowances or leave. Several traditions none the less distinguish them from other ratings. They wear white badges, not red ones, on all blue uniforms and, contrary to normal naval practice, they tuck their jumpers *inside* their trousers, thus displaying the black silk bow at the back of each waistband. They wear white plimsolls, so that the noise of their footsteps on deck is reduced to a royal hush, and in keeping with the atmosphere of a hotel, on the upper decks orders are indicated by hand signals or are softly spoken. Aft of the mainmast ratings go without their hats – to spare the royal passengers the ever-recurring obligation of returning sailors' salutes.

The royal apartments occupy all four decks in the rear half of the ship. They include a wine-cellar, strongroom, a lift, and a garage for a royal Rolls-Royce. The royal galley and pantries are forward by the funnel, adjoining a 45-foot-long dining-room, where as many as fifty-six people may dine in style, seated on Hepplewhite chairs. Here also feature films can be shown from an up-to-date stock on a screen concealed by sliding panels. On the honeymoon cruise nine new films, including *Chariots of Fire*, were taken on board. Aft of the dining-room is an ante-room, opening onto the main sitting-room – furnished, like the rest of the royal apartments, by Sir Hugh Casson in the tasteful chintzy mode of a country mansion. Above them, on the top or shelter deck, are cabins for valet and dresser, a wardrobe, and the master bedrooms. Other bedroom suites, offices and cabins abound further down. The crew's quarters are by contrast very cramped, as in most White Ensign ships, but everything is extremely spick and span.

There is accommodation in the royal apartments for about fifty people – staff and guests. On the honeymoon cruise the royal couple were accompanied by an equerry (Major John Winter), a secretary (Francis Cornish, who should have been holidaying with his family), a valet, and a lady's maid.

In addition to the full crew of 277, twenty-seven members of the Royal Marines Band were on board to play anything from Abba to 'Also Sprach Zarathustra'; from symphonic, military and ballet music (as requested) to pop music. It is easy to imagine the romantic sight and sounds of *Britannia* at night, a floating honeymoon hotel for two, dreamily sailing along the North African coast while faint music filtered into the air from her lighted decks.

It is not so easy to understand how such a large ship managed to elude all airborne press and photographic attention for virtually two weeks. The Mediterranean is, however, much larger than imagined, and *Britannia* swifter than her given top speed of 22.5 knots. At night she covered many miles undetected, turning up at daytime in some out-of-the-way and quite unexpected places. Expected ports-of-call included Majorca, Sardinia, Tangier, Malta (where the Prince spent a holiday for the first time without his parents in 1968), Naples and Cyprus.

The Royal Yacht, in fact, headed southeastwards through the night from Gibraltar towards Algeria, and for two days (2 and 3 August) meandered eastwards along the Algerian coast. The couple spent their time soaking up the sun and sea air and more than likely bathing in a canvas makeshift swimming-pool. They would also now have had a chance to watch the video-tape recordings of their wedding day which had been brought on board the ship at Gibraltar.

On 5 August *Britannia*, now sailing off the northern shores of Tunisia, turned towards Sicily. She cruised around the north of the island, past the Isles of Lipari and the volcanic island of Stromboli, before sailing down through the Straits of Messina on Thursday, 6 August. The following morning, 7 August, an Italian frigate, the *Sagittario*, that had shadowed *Britannia*'s passage through Italian waters, steamed up as the Royal Yacht moved into the Ionian Sea. The frigate's sailors lined her decks and cheered as the two ships passed and went their separate ways.

The Royal Yacht moved on into Greek coastal waters. That evening, a hundred miles south of Corfu, where Prince Philip was born in June 1921, she anchored off the mountainous island of Ithaca, the home of the ancient Greek hero, Odysseus. The couple went ashore by launch, to a secluded beach where they swam for an hour or two as the sun set. The Ithacan town of Vathi had been decorated with bunting and flags and a welcoming party had been prepared by the mayor, but the honeymooners, still loath to face any crowds, made no public appearances. However, on Saturday morning, before *Britannia* sailed, they found time to call at the luxurious villa of Constantine Gratsos, 77-year-old president of the Onassis shipping-line, to thank him for the use of his beach the night before.

Meanwhile, a gunboat of the Greek Navy kept unobtrusive watch for press photographers who might descend on the couple from air, sea or land. Governments had been informed in advance of *Britannia*'s movements and her route was kept under discreet surveillance by the ships and planes of other nations. An intrusive helicopter carrying pressmen was warned off by the gunboat and the privacy of the honeymooners remained undisturbed.

LEFT: *One of the few sightings of the Royal Yacht during the honeymoon – seen here in Greek waters off the Peloponnese.*
RIGHT: *On 12 August* Britannia *moored off Port Said in Egypt, at the northern end of the Suez Canal.*

But the threat of press invasion was enough to make *Britannia* curtail her stay. That afternoon she moved on, sailing southwards past Cephalonia, Zante, the Peloponnese and Kithira to Crete. On Sunday she anchored off the northwest point of Crete, at Grabousa, and once again the honeymooners went ashore by launch, seeking a beach inaccessible by land and far from the eyes of the curious. They picnicked and swam, enjoying a barbecued meal on the beach that moonlit night.

On Monday, 10 August, *Britannia* sailed northeast, so that the couple could inspect the Greek island of Santorini, formerly called Thira, whose cataclysmic volcanic annihilation some 3,500 years ago led to the destruction of the Minoan civilization on Crete and the creation of the legend of Atlantis. The crater-like cliffs of Santorini now half surround a very deep bay and the low island of an active volcanic cone.

From here the ship moved eastwards, cruising through the Greek islands of the Dodecanese, past Rhodes, and eventually made her way south to Egypt and Port Said.

She moored a hundred yards off Port Said (to the general frustration of press photographers) late on the afternoon of Wednesday, 12 August. Police launches kept boatloads of sightseers well away. The Princess, wearing a blouse, bermuda shorts and a straw hat, could be seen for a time on the bridge with Prince Charles (in shirt and shorts) before they went below.

That night the governor of Port Said laid on a hastily assembled firework display. Earlier, President Anwar Sadat and his English-born wife, Jihan, accompanied by the British Ambassador, Sir Michael Weir, were entertained to dinner by the Prince and Princess on board *Britannia*. After dinner the President presented the Prince with one of Egypt's highest honours, the Order of the Republic, First Class.

Britannia weighed anchor soon after midnight and then began a slow passage through the 103 miles of the Suez Canal and its interconnecting lakes, which the royal couple saw at dawn on 13 August. The Royal Yacht, heading a large convoy of vessels that included an Egyptian minesweeper, stopped for a while in the Great Bitter Lake to allow a convoy advancing up the Canal to pass. Prince Charles who, it seems, had thought of water-skiing here, changed his mind: there were too many ships and observers. Instead, he and his wife sunbathed on the upper deck, she in a yellow bikini. *Britannia* eventually emerged from the Canal at 2 p.m., steaming into the Gulf of Suez, past Suez itself, and out into the Red Sea.

The relaxed and sun-tanned Princess wore a straw hat with bermuda shorts and a matching blouse when Britannia *moored off Port Said.*

On Friday, 14 August, the Royal Yacht anchored off Shadwan Island, midway between the African coast of Egypt and the Sinai Peninsula. The honeymooners spent all day here, swimming from a sandy beach in the warm, clear waters of the Red Sea. It was immensely hot. The Prince went snorkelling and scuba-diving, exploring the coral reefs alive with legions of brightly coloured fish. Some of the crew went fishing and caught a shark. Friday night was the last that the royal couple spent on *Britannia*.

The following morning the Royal Yacht headed twenty miles south to the African coast. She moored offshore and a launch brought the Prince and Princess to Hurghada, a burgeoning resort on the Red Sea. Looking fit and tanned they stepped ashore and were driven two miles to an Egyptian airfield on the edge of the Eastern Desert, where the temperature was 100°F. President and Madame Sadat, who had flown down specially from Alexandria in the presidential Boeing 737, greeted them before bidding them farewell. After Prince Charles had inspected a helmeted guard of honour, he and his young wife entered the RAF VC10 that would take them home. At the top of the stairs leading into the aircraft the Princess turned towards the President and his wife and blew them a kiss.

After a six-hour flight, the VC10 landed at 4.35 p.m. at RAF Lossiemouth in Morayshire, Scotland, and was greeted by hundreds of RAF personnel and their families. From here Prince Charles drove the Princess to Balmoral Castle for a reunion with his parents and her sister, Lady Jane. The honeymoon was over. The Princess's Scottish summer holiday had just begun – her first as a member of the royal family, and as a married woman. Before it ended she would also become a mother-to-be.

CHAPTER THREE

Princess of Wales

DESPITE HER TITLE, the Princess will pass far more of her time in Scotland than in Wales. Every summer from now on she and her husband will spend August and September in the Grampian mountains on the Queen's 24,000-acre Balmoral estates on either side of the River Dee. This is in addition to the social and royal visits they will make annually to Scotland. She is no stranger to England's northern neighbour.

For since 1972 she has often spent holidays with her mother and her stepfather, Peter Shand Kydd, on the Isle of Seil, where the Shand Kydds have a 1,000-acre hill-farm. Mother and daughter are both very fond of the Scots and Scotland: the Princess's grandmother Ruth, Lady Fermoy, is Scottish – as is the Queen Mother, grandmother of the Prince. Lady Fermoy, whose father was Colonel William Gill, was brought up

LEFT: *The Prince and Princess of Wales gave an unprecedented photocall to the press by the Brig o' Dee on the Balmoral estate on 19 August 1981.*

BELOW: *Balmoral Castle, with its 17,400-acre estate, was bought by Queen Victoria and Prince Albert in 1852. It remains the Scottish home of the royal family.*

at Bieldside, not far from Aberdeen and some ninety miles east of Balmoral.

On the northern side of the River Dee, opposite Balmoral Castle, is Crathie Church. Here, on Sunday, 16 August 1981, the morning after the Princess and her husband left Egypt by plane, she made a public but unofficial appearance – a very brief one, as the royal cars drove right up to the church door. The sermon, preached by the Right Reverend Andrew Doig, Moderator of the Church of Scotland, was prophetically based on the text, 'Go and bear fruit'. Thousands of people who had flooded into the area to see the Princess, as well as scores of press photographers, caught little more than a glimpse of her.

To satisfy the press and ensure some privacy over the rest of their holiday, the couple agreed to pose informally for the media three days later. So, on a damp, dull and cloudy Wednesday morning, thirty photographers, twenty journalists and two television crews assembled at the Brig o' Dee. They were met by Palace press and police officers and instructed to gather across the bridge on the south bank of the river. Some photographers had suggested that the Prince might be pictured doing some fishing, assisted by his wife, but when the honeymooners appeared at ten o'clock, he carried no fishing tackle. Having arrived in a Range Rover, which was parked out of sight, the couple walked through the heather towards the horde of pressmen with the romantic old bridge behind them. There was a rapid fire of motor-driven Nikons, as the first snaps of a fine set of pictures were taken, later much approved by the Palace.

The Princess was wearing a brown houndstooth suit; the Prince a well-worn lovat-mixture jersey and a Royal Hunting Stewart kilt, once worn by George VI. They were both tanned and cheerful, and confidently faced the cameras.

Prince Charles was in a bantering, jovial mood. He inquired, 'Where do you want us to perform?' Obligingly, the couple posed for pictures by the wooden rail of a fisherman's rest – 'This must be very exciting television,' he suggested – showing a remarkable physical awareness of each other; a closeness and a naturalness that made the photographers' task easy.

Replying to reporters' queries, the Prince said, 'It's marvellous to be up here in Scotland – it's about 40 degrees cooler than the Red Sea. Much better . . . I hope you had a nice time going around the Mediterranean.' When he was asked whether he had been fishing for salmon in the Dee, he answered, 'No, the water's far too low.'

For the photocall by the Brig o' Dee the Princess wore a houndstooth suit designed by Bill Pashley and shoes from The Chelsea Cobbler.

The Princess was asked how her fishing lessons were getting along. 'Slowly,' she replied. To other questions about being married she answered, 'I can highly recommend it.' But a more particular question about whether she had yet cooked breakfast for her husband produced the retort, 'I don't eat breakfast.' Before her engagement she had been friendly, almost familiar, with the press; now she gave little away – except the fact that she was immensely happy.

When a local lady journalist presented the Princess with a cellophane-wrapped bouquet of flowers (suggested by the photographers and paid for by a whip-round among the press), the Princess said, 'Thank you very much,' adding with a teasing laugh, 'I bet these come off your expenses.' The presentation was, however, too premature, as several photographers wanted still more pictures, and the bouquet had to be temporarily retrieved. As requested, the couple now strolled down to the riverside, where the Prince gallantly kissed his wife's hand and put his arm around

The Princess went shopping more than once in nearby Ballater with her husband's aunt, Princess Margaret, accompanied here by one of the Queen's ladies-in-waiting, Lady Susan Hussey.

her. Invariably somewhat self-conscious when on display, he was on this occasion less so than ever before and unusually demonstrative. The photographers were well pleased when after fifteen minutes the photo session ended.

Prince Charles, realizing the value his young wife put on her personal freedom – as a commoner living in a London flat she had been accustomed to much freedom of movement and choice – was anxious for her to do more or less as she pleased. In the ensuing weeks, when he went out grouse-shooting on the moors or fly-fishing for salmon in the River Dee, she sometimes went with him, joining him for a packed lunch. At other times she rambled along the river and about the main Balmoral estate, her chief companion being Lady Sarah Armstrong-Jones, then aged seventeen and a half and since the wedding a firm friend. They went shopping together in Ballater, where Lady Sarah's mother, Princess Margaret (who had arrived at Balmoral after her 51st birthday on 21 August), was able to give the Princess of Wales some good advice about antiques. However, a coal-scuttle was apparently all that she bought.

The Princess's own family were at hand to share in the happiness of her married life. Lady Jane Fellowes,

with her husband and their daughter, Laura, aged two, was staying in a lodge near Balmoral Castle. As the Queen's Assistant Private Secretary, Robert Fellowes was on a working holiday. At Birkhall, from 27 August, Lady Fermoy was in attendance on the Queen Mother as her lady-in-waiting, both having spent the previous weeks at the Castle of Mey near John o' Groats. Mrs Shand Kydd and her husband Peter also stayed at Balmoral at the end of August as guests of the Queen. Later, the Princess was visited by her elder sister, Lady Sarah McCorquodale, by her brother, Charles and former flatmates, Virginia Pitman and Carolyn Pride.

It was very much a family holiday and the Princess revelled in her new-found status as a wife. Although she had been a guest at Balmoral twice before, her status as the daughter-in-law of the Queen and Prince Philip was also something to be enlarged on and enjoyed by all. Prince Philip is said to have joked with

On 5 September the royal family attended the Royal Braemar Gathering. Since the wedding, Lady Sarah Armstrong-Jones (on the right) has become a firm friend of the Princess, who on this occasion wore a red and black plaid wool and cotton suit, piped with black Russian braid, and designed by Caroline Charles.

Competitive events at the annual Braemar Games which began in 1832 include Highland dancing.

her about that moment during the wedding service when she mixed up the bridegroom's names, putting *his* first. Her sense of humour, youth and candour much appealed to him, and as his only daughter, Princess Anne, was now immersed in her own life and children, he found his daughter-in-law's company a good substitute and great fun.

An example of the unusual degree of independence allowed the Princess came when on Wednesday, 2 September, she flew to London for a few days without her husband. Accompanied by a police officer, Graham Smith (and calling herself Mrs Smith), she travelled on the mid-morning scheduled British Airways flight from Aberdeen to Heathrow Airport, London. Staying at Buckingham Palace, she chose some new clothes and hats, had her hair done, called on friends, visited Highgrove to see how and where some of the wedding presents could best be fitted in, and toured the exhibition of those wedding presents that were on display in St James's Palace.

She returned to Balmoral in time for the royal family's annual outing to the Royal Braemar Gathering on Saturday, 5 September. Although she could have worn the Balmoral tartan, she chose to wear a severely buttoned-up textiled plaid suit and a black tam o' shanter. The royal party included the Queen, the Queen Mother, Prince Philip, Prince Charles, Viscount Linley and Lady Sarah Armstrong-Jones. They seated themselves in the royal box, and watched various competitive events including races, Highland dancing, piping, tossing the caber, pole-vaulting, hammer-throwing, sack races and a tug-of-war. More than once the Princess delightedly applauded the contestants. She was in such high spirits that when the national anthem was played, an unconsidered giggle drew a look from the Queen. Prince Charles is believed to have been the real miscreant, having jokingly whispered to his wife as they stood to attention, 'They're playing our song . . .'

That year Prince Charles did not, as he had done before his marriage, play polo at Scone Racecourse in Perthshire, although he went away on two occasions, paying official visits to Glasgow and Edinburgh. A highlight of the Queen's Balmoral holiday was the traditional Gillies' Ball, which was attended by every member of the Royal Family and held in the main hall of the Castle.

On Monday, 21 September, the Queen, Prince Philip and their households returned to London before beginning a royal tour of Australia, New Zealand and Sri Lanka; they would be away until the third week of October. On their departure from Scotland, Balmoral Castle was closed down, and the Prince of Wales and his wife moved into a large and comfortable lodge on the estate – Craigowan, near the royal nine-hole golf-course. Here they were at home over the next month to some of their own friends, whom they had not seen since the wedding. Once the Princess gamely went deer-stalking in the mountains. She shot, and cleanly killed, a stag. Not for the first time either, it appears. In the nursery at Althorp, her family home, is a pair of antlers tagged *D. Spencer*.

Shooting of another kind suddenly shattered the couple's Scottish holiday when they heard on 6 October of the assassination of President Anwar Sadat in Egypt. The Princess was much distressed by this. She is believed to have wept, saying, 'It's terrible, so terrible. How can people behave like that?' The President, the only foreign head of state she had met – and entertained on her honeymoon in her own right as Princess of Wales – had been shot and killed by some of his own troops.

When it was decided that Prince Charles should attend the state funeral of President Sadat in Cairo, her emotions must have been very mixed. She wished to go with him out of respect for the dead President and his widow, and to be near her husband. But Foreign Office diplomats could not allow this, nor was it possible for a woman to attend Muslim obsequies. However, she travelled with Prince Charles to London on Friday, 9 October, and went to Heathrow Airport to see him off. It was their first real parting, and she could not help fearing for his own safety in Egypt, despite the biggest security operation ever mounted in Cairo. At the steps of the VC10, she kissed the Prince, patted his arm and wiped the tears from her eyes.

But the following night they were safely reunited at Buckingham Palace before flying back to Craigowan. Perhaps it was then – so often is a death followed by a life – that she told him she might be going to have a baby. For within a few days – while the Prince visited Birmingham and the scenes of recent riots in Toxteth, Liverpool – she was back in London.

On Wednesday, 14 October, she drove from Heathrow to Highgrove to finalize furniture arrangements as well as the disposition of the wedding gifts previously displayed at St James's Palace (where the London Exhibition had ended on 4 October). On returning to London she called on Vicky Wilson and Kath Seth-Smith at the Young England Kindergarten. It is most probable that on this crowded one-day visit she also went to see the Queen's Surgeon Gynaecologist, Mr George Pinker, for an examination.

Two of the Prince's skiing friends, Charles and Patty Palmer-Tomkinson, holidaying at Craigowan, were among the first to realize that the Princess was pregnant. They were told she would not be skiing with them at Klosters in February. The fact that she might be expecting did not stop the Princess from throwing herself into an extempore party for estate workers on 16 October. Wearing a tartan sash over a long white evening dress, she danced reels, strathspeys and 'disco' numbers. At one point she is said to have sat on the floor and complained, 'My feet are killing me – it's because my shoes are new.'

The couple's Scottish holiday, that had made up the major part of their three-month sojourn, ended on Sunday, 25 October. In the morning they attended the

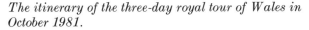

The itinerary of the three-day royal tour of Wales in October 1981.

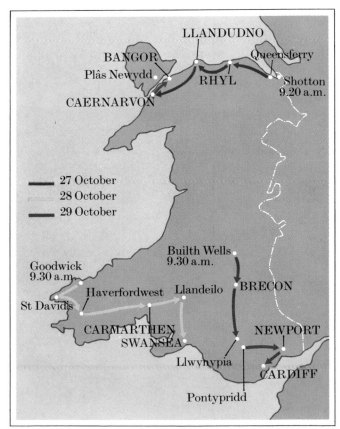

The Princess was received enthusiastically by the people of Rhyl. Her wool crêpe suit in red and green, the Welsh national colours, was designed by Donald Campbell. She wore matching red shoes from Rayne.

service at Crathie Church and that evening flew back to London and returned to Buckingham Palace. The Queen and Prince Philip also flew back to London from Colombo that day, at the end of their overseas tour, and heard their daughter-in-law's glad news.

Thus it was that the royal tour of Wales by the Prince and Princess of Wales began in a mood of secret celebration on Tuesday, 27 October. It was their first official appearance together in public since their wedding in St Paul's Cathedral on 29 July, and it was the first time that the Princess had ever been to Wales. She and her husband share Owen Glendower, the last Welsh Prince of Wales, as an ancestor. But although Prince Charles is now the twenty-first British

Prince of that nation, among all his possessions he owns nothing in Wales itself.

During the Welsh tour – timed to coincide with half-term holidays from school – the royal couple covered hundreds of miles and went on ten 'walkabouts'. At night they slept on the air-conditioned Royal Train occupying two new Royal Saloons, which came into service in 1977, the year of the Queen's Silver Jubilee.

The three-day tour, keenly anticipated by most of the Welsh people, began at 9.20 a.m. in North Wales at Shotton railway station, where the Prince and Princess left the Royal Train and were driven in a large, glass-backed Rolls-Royce to Rhyl, a grey little seaside resort. It was a cold, dull day with a bitter wind. Their first day's gruelling schedule included visits to Llandudno, Caernarvon, Bangor and Plas Newydd. After showing some nervous diffidence (natural for a twenty-year-old girl) while dignitaries were introduced to her, the Princess plunged into her first and unexpectedly

ABOVE: *Mr Walter Hill, aged fifty-one, who suffers from multiple sclerosis, was overcome at meeting the new Princess of Wales in Rhyl, but she waited until he could express his pleasure at seeing her.*
RIGHT: *The visit to Caernarvon Castle was one of the highlights of the tour. The castle was the scene of Prince Charles's Investitute as Prince of Wales on 1 July 1969.*

enjoyable walkabout. Right from the start, wearing the Welsh colours of red and green, she purposefully went about the business of meeting the people. As the Prince advanced down one side of the street with considered ease, keeping a slight distance from the clutching crowds, on the other side his wife was almost being hauled over the barriers, letting her ungloved hand be grasped by hundreds of well-wishers and fans. She was an object of wonder and much affection, as both a Princess, Superstar and the young and beautiful wife of the most popular member of a well-regarded royal family – most popular, that is, until she superceded him. 'Isn't she lovely!' women exclaimed, avidly eyeing her face and dress. 'Ooh. Isn't she tall! I had no idea!'

Posies that were eagerly given to her were passed to her lady-in-waiting and amassed in the arms of policewomen. The Prince was more than once asked to give proffered bunches of flowers to his wife across the road. 'Diana,' he called, 'over here.' He grinned. 'I'm very good at collecting flowers for my wife,' he remarked. When spectators asked for her, he remarked, 'I'm sorry there's only one of her. I haven't got enough wives to go around.' On one occasion a middle-aged man in a wheelchair, overcome by meeting her, burst into tears. She waited, patiently concerned, until he recovered and was able to speak to her, before she moved on.

At Queensferry, on that first day, the Prince opened the Deeside Leisure Centre, where he and his wife listened to a harpist and a children's choir. At Llandudno they had a buffet lunch prepared by the catering

students of the local technical college. Reporters and press photographers who were covering the tour – over nine hundred had applied for press passes – raced ahead to Caernarvon. Prince Charles had originally intended to pay a private visit to Caernarvon Castle, to show his wife where he had been invested as Prince of Wales in 1969. But when permission was sought for children to meet and greet them there, it was granted.

They were met at the Castle by Lord Snowdon, repeating his role at the Investiture as the Castle's Constable. They went inside to the great central arena, fringed with motley groups of guides, scouts and majorettes. By now the Princess was wearing a pair of black gloves to protect her hands, raw with the cold and hundreds of handshakes. Overhead, the sinking sun gilded the battlements and local children sang a folk song in Welsh. For some reason the couple, distanced on awkward stools on the slate dais, seemed anxious, even ill at ease. Perhaps some security problem troubled them – a small group of Welsh nationalists, bent on creating disturbances, demonstrated throughout the tour. More probably, the Princess's discomfort, at being an isolated, inactive target for staring eyes, communicated itself to her husband. When she appeared with him on a high castle balcony overlooking the square, where he as Prince of Wales had been presented by his mother to the people, some similar alarm or the gusting wind, or the height above the crowds, made her take a nervous step backwards.

An hour later, a noisy stink-bomb demonstration, obscured by cheering crowds, resulted in scuffles and arrests. But the day ended with a calmer reception in Plas Newydd, home of the Marquess of Anglesey and now run by the National Trust. Here a lavish buffet was barely touched by the couple as they dutifully circulated among the invited guests. Later, no doubt tired by the peculiar strain of being on show all day, they dined quietly together on the Royal Train.

The Prince of Wales informally presented his wife, the Princess of Wales, to the Welsh people at Caernarvon Castle on 27 October 1981.

RIGHT: *On 28 October the royal couple visited the smallest city in Britain, to attend a bilingual service at St David's Cathedral on its 800th anniversary. The Princess wore a cashmere coat over a matching pleated skirt and a cream silk blouse. The outfit was designed by Caroline Charles and the hat by John Boyd.*

BELOW: *Despite the rain, the Princess was determined not to disappoint anybody at Llandeilo although she became rather wet during the visit.*

The Prince and Princess were welcomed by excited crowds at Haverfordwest before another walkabout in the rain.

The second day of the tour was spent in the south, beginning at Goodwick, then on to St David's, where the 800th anniversary of the cathedral, built on the site of the monastery of Wales's patron saint, was being celebrated. The weather was still foul, but the large crowds were even more demonstrative than the day before, and on entering the cathedral precincts the couple seemed surprised and delighted by such a warm response on a cold October morning.

Again they divided their attentions between the people lining both sides of the path to the cathedral. Prince Charles seemed to revel even more in his wife's great personal success. No longer the centre of attention himself, he was able to relax completely, and chatted easily with local people and visitors. As he talked, however, he kept a cautious eye on his wife, constantly ready to reassure and save her from the more voracious spectators. 'Come along,' he would say. 'We don't want to be late.'

After listening to a bilingual service in the cathedral, the Prince and Princess were driven to Haverfordwest, where in pouring rain there was another walkabout – and then yet another at Carmarthen. Here they also stopped for lunch in the local technical college. The continuing rain neither dampened the crowd's enthusiasm nor the Princess's energy, either at Carmarthen or at the next stop, Llandeilo. She seemed bent on ensuring that the people and children who had waited for hours in the rain should not be disappointed.

Photographer Tim Graham, who exhaustively covered the three-day tour, said of the second day: 'There was an incredible turnout to meet her in some really terrible weather. It must have been quite an ordeal for the Princess in terms of the sheer number of people wanting to shake her hand and yelling at her. At times she held out her left hand, the other had been gripped so much. Sometimes her smile became rather fixed – but that's inevitable. It can't be easy having to be a charming, chatty person all day. But she was fantastic with the kids. She would often kneel down to talk to them – something no other Royal would do. At Carmarthen she spotted a couple of small children trying to peer through some railings and obviously not doing very well. So she went over to them and chatted to them both for a while and made their day. Then at Pontypridd she noticed two little kids bawling their

ABOVE: *At Carmarthen, the Princess cheered up the children who had been waiting to see her in the cold wet weather.*
RIGHT: *On the other side of the street, Prince Charles collected flowers for his wife.*

heads off. She promptly went over and took a chocolate bar out of her pocket and gave them a piece each. One stopped crying at once, but the other didn't. So the Princess wrapped the other piece of chocolate up and dropped it in the child's pocket.'

That night the Princess dazzled the guests at a gala concert performed by three hundred young musicians and dancers in the Brangwyn Hall, Swansea. She arrived in a black velvet cape over a green tafetta ball-gown, wearing an emerald necklace. Outside, a small bunch of demonstrators bearing placards saying, *English Royalty Go Home* and *Fight for a Welsh Republic*, chanted, 'Prince out! Prince out!' Inside the hall a choir sang, 'God bless the Prince of Wales,' adding 'God bless the Princess too.'

On the third and final day of the tour, Thursday, 29 October, the royal couple visited Builth Wells, Brecon, Llwynypia Hospital in the Rhondda, Ponty-pridd, Newport and Cardiff. Again it rained. In the maternity ward of the hospital, it was evident that the Princess found the crush of television cameras and attendant photographers displeasing. It was Prince Charles, like a seasoned television personality, who did as he was expected to do – passing around the beds, chatting and joking with apparent ease. He asked a young mother whether her husband had been present at the birth. When she replied, 'Yes,' he commented,

LEFT: *At Cardiff, the Princess received the Freedom of the City at a ceremony in the City Hall, when she made her first speech, part of it in Welsh. She wore a blue and gold striped chiffon dress by Donald Campbell.*
ABOVE LEFT: *The Prince and Princess were the principal guests at a Gala Concert at Brangwyn Hall in Swansea on 28 October, when the Prince announced that the Mayor of Swansea would be elevated to the status of Lord Mayor. The Princess wore a green taffeta dress from Nettie Vogues and a black velvet cape by Gina Fratini.*

ABOVE RIGHT: *The last day of the Welsh tour took the royal couple to Brecon, where the sun shone for a while. The Princess wore another stylish hat by John Boyd and a burgundy velvet suit from Jaeger.*

'I think it's a very good thing for husbands to be with their wives when they're having a baby.'

The Welsh tour ended that night at Cardiff City Hall when the Princess was presented with the Freedom of the City, after which she made her first-ever speech. Dressed in glittering blue chiffon, she said, speaking in an uncharacteristically rapid monotone and reading from a script:

I am extremely grateful to you, Lord Mayor, and to the City Council and to the City of Cardiff for granting me the Freedom of the City. I realize that this is a very great honour and I am most grateful. I would like to try to express my thanks to you in Welsh also. *Y mae'n bleser cael dod i Cymru. Hoffwn ddod eto yn fuan. Diolch yn fawr.* I do hope that bore some relationship to what I meant to say – which is basically that it is a very great pleasure for me to come to Wales, and to its capital, Cardiff. I look forward to returning many times in the future. Also I'd like just to add how proud I am to be Princess of such a beautiful place and of the Welsh people, who are very special to me.

Her speech was greeted with rapturous applause. Prince Charles smiled. He could feel well-pleased with his wife, and himself. Having studied Welsh for one term at Aberystwyth University, he had been able to help her with her Welsh pronunciation as well as the wording of the speech, and for a modest young girl she had coped with everything extraordinarily well.

A week later, at the Guildhall in London, on the day that it was announced that the Princess was expecting a baby in June, the Prince said that the three-day tour of Wales had been 'overwhelming – and entirely due to the effect of my dear wife.'

CHAPTER FOUR

Predecessors

IN THE 680 YEARS since the first Prince of Wales was invested with that title at Lincoln in 1301 – Prince Charles is the twenty-first – there have been only eight Princesses of Wales.

The most glamorous was Joan, *the first Princess of Wales* and wife of the second Prince of Wales, Edward of Woodstock; the eldest son of Edward III, he was nicknamed the Black Prince after his death. He was also the first Englishman to be ennobled as a Duke, as the first Duke of Cornwall.

The first Prince of Wales, the ill-fated Edward II, was in fact an uncle of Lady Joan – her father, Edmund, Earl of Kent, being the son of Edward I by his second marriage. The Earl of Kent died in 1330, two years after his daughter Joan was born; and when her mother, Margaret Wake, died in 1352, Joan became Countess of Kent in her own right. Such was her beauty – she was known as the Fair Maid of Kent – she acquired many admirers at court, where she was brought up in the Queen's household. It was a very sporty, colourful court: heraldry and tournaments were in their heyday and chivalry in full bloom. Europe's oldest order of chivalry, the Order of the Garter, dates from this time – from a legendary incident at a ball held to celebrate the fall of Calais in 1347, when the King is said to have picked up a garter lost by the eighteen-year-old Fair Maid of Kent herself and remarked, '*Honi soit qui mal y pense*' – 'Shamed be he who thinks ill of this.'

Joan of Kent had by then been twice married. She first secretly married the Earl of Salisbury's steward, Sir Thomas Holland. This displeased the court politicians, including the King. Sir Thomas was dispatched to the fighting in France, and his young wife was married to the Earl of Salisbury's heir. When Sir Thomas returned from the French wars late in the year 1347,

he demanded that his wife be restored to him. The Pope's judgment was sought and decided in his favour. Joan, Countess of Salisbury, became Lady Holland once more. She bore Sir Thomas five children, returning with him to France, where he died in 1360 after taking part in peace treaty negotiations at Brétigny. Nine months later she married the Prince of Wales: she was thirty-two.

They had known each other since childhood. The Prince was two years younger than his beautiful cousin. His father had wanted him to make a political match and marry the widowed heiress of the Duke of

LEFT: *The ninth Princess of Wales. The first official portrait of Lady Diana Spencer, fiancée of the Prince of Wales. Painted by Bryan Organ, 1981.*
RIGHT: *Joan of Kent, wife of the Black Prince, and first Princess of Wales (1328–85).*

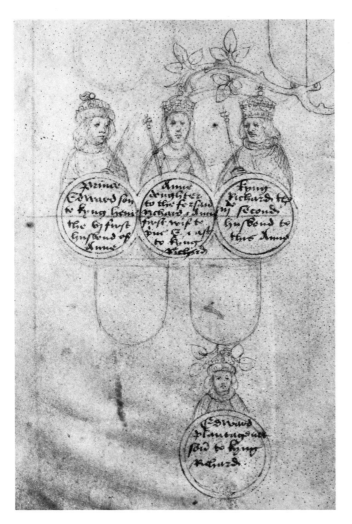

Lady Anne Neville, daughter of Richard, Earl of Warwick, married Edward, the fifth Prince of Wales in 1470. He was killed in 1471, and the following year she married the Duke of Gloucester, later Richard III (on the right). Their only child, Edward, born in 1473, died in 1484, before his parents.

Burgundy. Instead, he married his cousin, another wealthy widow. It seems that despite paternal pressure on him to marry and produce male heirs, he had waited until the Fair Maid was free. Their opulent wedding took place in the new Garter Chapel of St George in Windsor on 10 October 1361.

Created Duke of Aquitaine, the Prince marched off in 1362 with his wife to France, to Bordeaux, where she bore him two sons: Edward, who died within a few years, and Richard.

The Prince of Wales, ill with dropsy and heavily in debt, returned to England in January 1371, to his manor at Berkhamsted. His reputation had been smudged by his last military exploit, the destruction of Limoges, where over three thousand citizens were slaughtered. In England he dwindled away and five

years later he died: he was forty-six. The following year, in July 1377, his widow, the Princess of Wales – a month after the death of the old king, Edward III – saw her surviving son, aged ten, crowned at Westminster as Richard II.

Over the next eight years she witnessed little else that was glorious, as the age of chivalry became debased. The peasantry rebelled and the boy king's uncles, earls and barons fought among themselves. She died on 7 August 1385, at the age of fifty-seven.

The second Princess of Wales was the youngest to marry and the youngest to die. Born in 1456, Lady Anne Neville, daughter of Richard, Earl of Warwick (the Kingmaker), was fourteen when she was betrothed to the only child of Henry VI in July 1470. Her husband, the fifth Prince of Wales, Edward of Lancaster, was sixteen – 'a goodly feminine and well-featured young gentleman'. The ceremony took place in Angers Cathedral and cemented an uneasy alliance between the Earl of Warwick and the Lancastrians, headed by the redoubtable wife of King Henry VI, Margaret of Anjou. On Easter Sunday, 1471, Queen Margaret landed with her son, Prince Edward, the Prince of Wales, at Weymouth. Her forces were caught by the Yorkist army at Tewkesbury. In the ensuing battle, on 4 May, the Lancastrians were overwhelmed and their cause lost. Queen Margaret was captured and the Prince of Wales butchered. Later that month, on the night of Edward IV's triumphant return to London, Henry VI was murdered in the Tower.

The teenage Anne, Princess of Wales, fatherless and widowed in less than a month, was married within a year of her husband's death to his enemy, her slight dark cousin, Richard, Duke of Gloucester, then aged eighteen. Early in 1473, aged sixteen, she gave birth to a son, Edward, at Middleham in Yorkshire. She bore no other children.

Ten years passed, and when in April 1483 Edward IV died, the 27-year-old Duchess of Gloucester was crowned with much magnificence in July alongside her murderous husband, Richard III.

He had won both crown and kingdom despite the existence of three boys with better claims to the throne: Edward V, aged twelve, eldest son of Edward IV and formerly the sixth Prince of Wales; his brother, Richard, aged nine; and the nine-year-old son of the Duke of Clarence, the new king's older brother, who had been tried for treason.

The two Princes were imprisoned in the Tower and murdered soon after the coronation of Richard III, when Edward of Middleham, the ten-year-old and only son of King Richard and Queen Anne, was invested at York as the next and seventh Prince of Wales. But in March the following year the young Prince (as the Croyland chronicler reports) 'in whom all

Catherine of Aragon (1486–1536), the third Princess of Wales, attributed to Houbraken after Holbein. She married two Princes of Wales, Prince Arthur and Prince Henry, later Henry VIII.

the hopes of the royal succession, fortified with so many oaths, were centred, was seized with an illness of but short duration and died at Middleham Castle . . . You might have seen his father and mother in a state almost bordering on madness, by reason of their sudden grief.'

A year later, on 16 March 1485, the now barren, unhappy Queen Anne herself died, aged twenty-seven – allegedly poisoned by her husband, who was anxious to remarry and breed sons to succeed him. But five months later Richard III, crying, 'Treason! Treason!' was killed at the Battle of Bosworth. His victor Henry Tudor became Henry VII and married Richard III's niece and prospective bride, Elizabeth of York.

Their two sons both married *the third Princess of Wales*, Catherine of Aragon. Born on 16 December 1485, the year in which her predecessor died, the Infanta Catalina was the youngest daughter of

Ferdinand, King of Spain, and Isabella of Castile. When she was two it was suggested that, to further an alliance between England and Spain, she should marry Arthur, the eighth Prince of Wales, who was then one year old.

They were eventually married by proxy in 1499, and the official ceremony took place in old St Paul's Cathedral on 14 November 1501, just before Princess Catherine's sixteenth birthday. The young bride, wearing a mantilla and a farthingale, unknown in England then, was escorted to the Cathedral by 'a hulking boy', the ten-year-old Henry, Duke of York (later Henry VIII). The wedding celebrations were sumptuous and extensive. Prince Arthur, who was over-educated and far from robust, was overcome by 'a sweating-sickness' when the teenage couple retired to Ludlow Castle in December. The Prince, aged fifteen, died a few months later on 2 April 1502. The marriage was never consummated, according to his widow.

Princess Catherine lived at court for the next seven years in obscure and abject poverty, eyed by the ageing Henry VII as a possible wife for political reasons, and by his youngest son, Henry, now the ninth Prince of Wales. When the old King died in April 1509, the young King proposed to Catherine and on 11 June, thirteen days before the coronation, the last Catholic Princess of Wales wed her husband's brother, Henry VIII. He was eighteen, she twenty-three.

They were married for nearly twenty-four years. Although she bore him seven children, four were miscarriages and two, both boys, lived for just a few weeks. The child who survived was her sixth, the Princess Mary (later Mary I). But the King wanted a son as his heir and planned that the mother should be his latest love, the vivacious Anne Boleyn. Queen Catherine was summoned to appear before a Papal Legative's court in the Great Hall of the Monastery of Blackfriars in June 1529 to determine the legality of her marriage. But it was not until May 1533 that the King, repudiating the authority of the Pope in Rome, managed to have the marriage declared null and void. Four months earlier he had secretly married Anne Boleyn. Their child, another daughter, Princess Elizabeth (later Elizabeth I), was born that September.

Queen Catherine, now the Dowager Princess of Wales, aged fifty, died of dropsy and heart disease at Kimbolton on 7 January 1536, and was buried in the Abbey of Peterborough. Four months later Queen Anne was tried for adultery and beheaded. The following day Henry VIII remarried. His third wife, Jane Seymour, bore him a son, but died in childbirth.

The fourth Princess of Wales was German. Princess Caroline of Brandenburg-Ansbach, daughter of the Margrave of Ansbach and orphaned in 1696 when she was thirteen, married Prince George Augustus of

Hanover ten years later. In 1714, on the death of Queen Anne and after Princess Caroline's boorish, middle-aged father-in-law became George I, her husband was invested as the fourteenth Prince of Wales.

There was not much apparent affection in the new royal family. Princess Caroline, a plumply extrovert, attractive, intelligent lady, forever denigrated but depended on by her husband, was described by the irascible George I as, 'That she-devil!' when she criticized his favourite Tory minister, Robert Walpole. The Prince and Princess of Wales associated with the opposition, the Whigs, lavishly entertaining them in Hampton Court Palace while the King was in Hanover – he had refused to make his son Regent in his absence. When George I returned, he had to be restrained from sending his eldest son to the Tower. Instead, the Prince and Princess were ordered out of Hampton Court and into a much smaller residence, Leicester House. They were forbidden to take their children with them.

Princess Caroline had eight children. She did not like her eldest child, Frederick Louis, who at the age of seven had been left behind in Hanover to be educated; there he remained until he was twenty-one. But when George I died, unlamented, in 1727, Frederick was brought over to England and invested as the fifteenth Prince of Wales in January 1729. His martial father, now George II, despised him. His militant mother, now Queen and made Regent in the King's absence, could hardly tolerate Prince Frederick's presence. But she was devoted in her fashion to her husband, George II, and he in his fashion doted on her. In 1737 on her death-bed, when she advised him to marry again, the King burst into tears and replied, between sobs: '*Non - j'aurais - des - maitresses.*' He slept on the floor at the foot of her bed in Kensington Palace until she died, at the age of fifty-four.

Queen Caroline's daughter-in-law, wife of Prince Frederick, was the German Princess Augusta of Saxe-Gotha, *the fifth Princess of Wales.* She was a tall, shy, gawky girl of seventeen, who spoke no English when she arrived in England in April 1736 to marry the Prince. The marriage was his father's idea. The Prince had planned to marry Lady Diana Spencer, granddaughter of the Dowager Duchess of Marlborough, thereby gaining a dowry of £100,000, which he needed to pay off his debts. But the King wanted his son and heir to marry a Princess, and preferably a German one.

Princess Augusta married her Prince in the Chapel Royal in St James's Palace on 26 April. Queen Caroline 'was obliged to explain to the Princess in the French or German tongue the marriage oath.' The Queen later described her daughter-in-law as 'far from beautiful' and said she had 'a wretched figure'.

This Princess of Wales bore more children than any other – nine. Indeed, her husband is said to have averred, 'A Prince should never talk to any woman of politics, or make use of any wife but to breed.' The Princess was carrying her ninth child, at the age of thirty-two, when in March 1751 Prince Frederick died, aged forty-three. A good father and a good husband, as well as an amiable sportsman and patron of the arts, the Prince was killed by a cricket-ball. It allegedly hit him and caused an abcess, which later burst after he caught a cold while gardening at Kew.

Princess Augusta ('Princess Prudence'), a prim, censorious woman and now Dowager Princess of Wales, was overwhelmed by her husband's sudden demise. Refusing to believe he was dead she sat by his corpse for more than a day. Then she wrote to her father-in-law, George II, commending herself and all her children to his 'paternal love and protection,' and when the King visited her he was met by her two eldest boys in a room entirely draped with black. The elder boy, twelve-year-old George William Frederick (later George III) was created Prince of Wales.

He became King in 1760 and married Princess Charlotte of Mecklenburg-Strelitz the following year.

LEFT: *Caroline of Ansbach when Princess of Wales. Her husband later became George II. Painting by the studio of Charles Jervas, pupil of Kneller, circa 1720.*
RIGHT: *Augusta, Princess of Wales. She married Prince Frederick, eldest son of George II, in 1736. Pastel on paper by Jean-Etienne Liotard, circa 1754.*

His mother, Princess Augusta, died, aged fifty-two, in February 1772 of cancer.

George III led an exemplary life with his wife, Queen Charlotte: he had no mistresses and she bore him fifteen children. The eldest, George Augustus Frederick, was born in August 1762 and became the seventeenth Prince of Wales five days later. However, it was fifty-eight years before he in turn became King as George IV. He was persuaded to marry a princess and to put aside his mistresses, provided that his debts, exceeding half a million pounds, were written off – as was his marriage to a Roman Catholic, Mrs Fitzherbert, for the Act of Settlement said the heir apparent forfeited the crown if married to a Catholic.

George III (eldest son of Prince Frederick) and Queen Charlotte with their six eldest children. The seventeenth Prince of Wales, Prince George, is on the left. The family are wearing 'Van Dyck' costumes for this portrait, painted by Zoffany in 1770.

Princess Caroline of Brunswick-Wolfenbüttel, *the sixth Princess of Wales*, was chosen by the King as a suitable bride despite some royal unease and the fact that she and the Prince were first cousins. The Queen had heard rumours of 'indecent conduct' involving the 26-year-old Princess and that this included 'indecent conversations with men'.

The Princess arrived in England with her mother (the King's elder sister) in April 1795. Her first meeting with the sixteen-stone, 32-year-old Prince, occurred a few days before their marriage. According to Lord Malmesbury, the Prince, after formally embracing his lumpy, malodorous fiancée, turned round, retired to a corner of the room and said, 'Harris, I am not well. Pray get me a glass of brandy.' At the wedding in St James's Palace he 'looked like death and was full of confusion' and 'had manifestly had recourse to wine or spirits.' The disgust of bride and groom was mutual. Later, Princess Caroline told a friend, 'Judge what it is to have a drunken husband on one's wedding day, and

one who spent the greater part of his bridal night under the grate, where he fell and I left him.' They formally separated after their only child, Princess Charlotte, was born in January 1796.

Princess Caroline, whose outspoken English was coloured by a German accent, was a coarse, shrewd and exhibitionistic woman, 'always seeking amusement and unfortunately,' according to Lady Charlotte Campbell, 'often at the expense of prudence and propriety.' In 1806, a 'Delicate Investigation' was instigated by the Prince into her affairs, both amorous and monetary, at her Blackheath residence. But no adultery could definitely be established, and the following year she moved into Kensington Palace, where she lived for seven years without modifying her opprobrious ways. In 1814 she went abroad, scandalizing Europe and the Middle East with her indecorous, eccentric dress and improper behaviour.

In May 1816, Princess Charlotte, only child of the Prince and Princess of Wales, married Prince Leopold of Saxe-Coburg-Saalfeld (later King of the Belgians) at Carlton House. He was tall, handsome, suave and poor. When he vowed, 'With all my wordly goods I thee endow,' the Princess laughed. She was not unlike her mother, being immodest, talkative, emotional, 'forward and dogmatical, buckish about horses and full of expressions very like swearing.' She looked 'rather like a young rascal dressed as a girl'. She conceived twice and miscarried. A third pregnancy resulted in a labour that lasted fifty hours – until on 4 November 1817 she was delivered of a dead boy. She died a few hours later, aged twenty-one.

The succession was suddenly imperilled, forcing the Prince of Wales to seek some means of divorcing his wife, so that he might remarry, and compelling his middle-aged younger brothers to set aside their mistresses and acquire acceptable wives. It was through his third brother, the Duke of Kent, that the crown passed to the Duke's daughter, Princess Victoria.

This marital agitation increased with the death, in January 1820, of George III. The Prince of Wales, now aged fifty-seven, became King as George IV. His wife, Princess Caroline, determined to be accepted as Queen, returned to England in June amid much vulgar acclaim. The King, even more determined to deprive her of her rights and titles and dissolve the marriage, instigated the first reading of a Bill of Pains and Penalties in the House of Lords on 5 July. It accused the Queen of conducting 'a licentious, disgraceful and adulterous intercourse' with Bartolommeo Pergami, her chamberlain and a former quartermaster. The public inquiry, attended by the Queen herself, began in August and dragged on until November, when the Bill was abandoned as the majority in favour was so small, and because – if the matter were raised in the

George, Prince of Wales (later George IV), characterized by George Cruikshank in this cartoon 'Thoughts on Matrimony' in 1795 at the time of his marriage. An oval miniature of his wife, Princess Caroline, hangs from his hand as he gazes at a portrait of his mistress, Lady Jersey. Beside the Prince stands a grotesque German courtier.

Commons – counter-accusations made against the King might well force him to abdicate.

Queen Caroline's popularity was now immense. Nevertheless, the Government decided that her name should be excluded from the Liturgy, and that she should not be crowned or live in a royal palace. When she brazenly drove in a State Landau, uninvited, to the coronation of George IV on 19 July 1821, the doors of Westminster Hall were closed in her face. She was told, 'There is no place for Your Majesty in the royal box or with the royal family.'

Shaken in spirit and in popularity, she fell ill, and died in great pain and delirium on 8 August. The King, who was on the Royal Yacht sailing to Ireland, paused at Holyhead, continuing with the voyage on 12 August, his fifty-ninth birthday. He landed in

Princess Charlotte, only child of the Prince and Princess of Wales, with her husband Prince Leopold of Saxe-Coburg-Saalfeld. When the princess died in childbirth in 1817, the succession was imperilled. Stipple engraving painted over in watercolour by William Thomas Fry, after George Dawe, 1817.

Ireland drunk, as the coffin of his dead Queen was shipped from Harwich to Germany, where she had asked to be buried. On the coffin was a plate, inscribed on her instruction, *Caroline of Brunswick: The Injured Queen of England*.

Queen Victoria's reign, from 1837 to 1901, lasted longer than that of any other British King or Queen, and her eldest son, Bertie (Prince Albert Edward, later Edward VII) was Prince of Wales for fifty-nine years, longer than any other. He married Princess Alexandra of Schleswig-Holstein-Sonderburg-Glucksburg, eldest daughter of Prince Christian, a captain in the Danish Guards. She became *the seventh Princess of Wales*.

Born on 1 December 1844, the Princess was eight when her father was made heir of the immoral and alcoholic Danish King, Frederick VII.

The Prince of Wales was barely nineteen when his mother and father began to consider which Protestant princess in Europe might be a suitable bride for him. They enlisted the aid of their eldest daughter, Vicky (already married to the Crown Prince of Prussia). Queen Victoria's main requirements were 'good looks,

health, education, character, intellect and a good disposition'. Princess Vicky duly reported home: Marie of Altenburg was 'shockingly dressed and always with her most disagreeable mother'; Marie of Hohenzollern was 'quite lovely' but a Catholic; Anna of Hesse had 'a rather gruff, abrupt way of speaking' and teeth 'nearly all spoilt'; Elizabeth of Weid had 'a great many freckles and a mark of a leaf on one cheek, but which does not show very much'; Alexandrine of Prussia was '*not* clever or pretty'. But of Alexandra of Denmark, whom she went to see, Vicky wrote: 'I never set eyes on a sweeter creature! She is lovely! . . . She is as simple and natural and unaffected as possible – and seems exceedingly well brought up.'

Although a marriage alliance with Denmark was not politically popular, and although Bertie had repeatedly said he would only marry for love, he travelled to the Rhineland with General Bruce to view the teenage Danish princess. Unknown to his parents, he was at that time enamoured of an actress, Nellie Clifden, by whom he had been recently and gladly seduced in a Grenadier Guards' summer camp near Dublin. At an arranged meeting in Speyer Cathedral on 24 September 1861, he and Princess Alexandra were introduced. Princess Vicky reported back to her mother: 'At first, I think, he was disappointed about her beauty and did not think her as pretty as he expected, but . . . in a quarter of an hour he thought her lovely . . . He said that he had never seen a young lady who pleased him so much . . . though her nose was too long and her forehead too low. She talked to him at first, in her simple and unaffected way. She was not shy. I never saw a girl of sixteen so forward for her age.'

The Prince told his mother that the young lady was 'charming and very pretty.' 'Oh, that boy!' wrote the Queen. 'As for being in love, I don't think he can be, or that he is capable of enthusiasm about anything in the world.' Prince Albert then had to tell her about her son's shocking enthusiasm for Nellie Clifden. The Prince Consort was deeply distressed by the 'disgusting details'. Tired and depressed, he caught a heavy cold and then typhoid. He died on 14 December that year.

The Queen blamed Bertie for her husband's death – 'I never can or shall look at him without a shudder' – but thought she might forgive him if he married the girl of whom Prince Albert had most approved. In September 1862, after the Queen had seen and thoroughly approved of Princess Alexandra herself, Bertie

Edward, Prince of Wales (Bertie), and Alexandra, seventh Princess of Wales, with two of their children – Prince Albert, who became engaged to Princess Victoria Mary of Teck, and Princess Maud. Painting by Von Angeli, 1876. Sandringham, where the painting hangs, can be seen in the background.

proposed in the bardens of the Palace of Laeken, near Brussels. He told his mother later, 'She immediately said, "Yes." But I told her not to answer too quickly but to consider over it. She said she had long ago. I then asked her if she liked me. She said, "Yes." I then kissed her hand and she kissed me.'

They were married in St George's Chapel, Windsor, on 10 March 1863. She was eighteen, he twenty-one. The mourning Queen wore black.

It was not until nearly fifty-eight years had passed that they became King and Queen, Edward VII reigning from January 1901 to his death on 6 May 1910. His wife, who stoically endured his self-indulgent gormandizing and gambling, and his amorous escapades with many other women, became increasingly unpunctual, eccentric, lame and deaf. She died at Sandringham on 20 November 1925, ten days before her eighty-first birthday.

Princess Alexandra had six children, the last being prematurely born and dying in April 1871 when she was twenty-six.

Her eldest son was Prince Albert Victor, Duke of Clarence, known to his family as 'Eddy'. His long neck, bony wrists, and dandified dress also earned him the nickname 'Collar and Cuffs'. This weak, slow-witted, sensual son drifted into an effetely dissipated life until his mother and grandmother, the Queen, decided in 1891 that he should marry a cousin, Princess Victoria Mary of Teck, who was then twenty-four-years old.

She was known as May and had been born in Kensington Palace on 26 May 1867, the only daughter of the German Duke of Teck and Princess Mary Adelaide (daughter of the Duke of Cambridge and grand-daughter of George III). According to Queen Victoria, May was 'a very nice girl, *distinguée*-looking, with a pretty figure.' She and her eldest brother were invited to stay at Balmoral in November 1891. Afterwards, the Queen wrote to her daughter Vicky (now Empress of Prussia): 'May is . . . so quiet and yet cheerful and so very carefully brought up and so sensible, I think and hope that Eddy will try and marry her.' He duly complied and proposed a few weeks later. Princess May wrote in her diary: 'To my great surprise Eddy proposed to me during the evening in Mme de Falbe's boudoir – Of course I said yes – We are both very happy.'

Princess Victoria Mary of Teck married Prince George, Duke of York, in the Chapel Royal at St James's Palace in July 1893. She became the eighth Princess of Wales. Queen Victoria is seen holding a fan in the centre (to the right) and the bride's mother, Princess Mary Adelaide, Duchess of Teck, opposite her in the foreground. Prince Albert (Eddy), the Princess's first fiancé, had died the year before. Painting by Laurits Tuxen.

The engagement was swiftly announced and the wedding arranged for 27 February 1892.

The royal family, at Sandringham for Christmas, was joined in the new year by Princess May and her parents in time for Eddy's twenty-eighth birthday on 8 January. He was sick with influenza, and five days later, having contracted pneumonia, he died, murmuring repeatedly, 'Who is that? Who is that? Who is that?' At his funeral, among the flowers upon his coffin, was a bridal wreath of orange blossom from his fiancée, Princess May.

In the spring, she was taken by her parents on holiday to the South of France – as was the new heir apparent, Eddy's younger brother, George, by *his* family. Prince George, Duke of York, had known Princess May nearly all his life. The young couple knew what was expected of them. On 3 May 1893 their engagement was announced.

During the eight-week engagement, the Princess wrote to her fiancé: 'This is a simply horrid time we are going through & I am only looking forward to the time when you & I shall be alone at Sandringham . . . I am very sorry that I am still so shy with you . . . I *love* you more than any body in the world & this I cannot tell you myself, so I write it to relieve my feelings.'

They were married in the Chapel Royal of St James's Palace on 6 July 1893. The future and *eighth Princess of Wales* was by then twenty-six. Queen Victoria, now seventy-four, wrote in her journal: 'Georgie gave his answers very distinctly, while May, though quite self-possessed, spoke very low . . . We got home before anyone else . . . went to the middle room, with the balcony, overlooking The Mall, and stepped out amidst much cheering. Very soon the Bride and Bridegroom arrived and I stepped out on the balcony with them, taking her by the hand.'

Prince George and his wife became Prince and Princess of Wales in 1901 after his father's accession to the throne; and when Edward VII died in 1910, they became King and Queen. They reigned until King George V died in January 1936.

Queen Mary lived on for many years, the most regal symbol and figure the nation had seen since Elizabeth I. She died on 24 March 1953, aged eighty-five.

She and King George V had six children: five sons and one daughter. Again it was the second son, another Duke of York, who suddenly found himself King when his elder borther, Edward VIII, formerly the twentieth Prince of Wales, abdicated at the end of 1936.

It was thirty-three years later, on 1 July 1969, that Prince Charles, eldest grandson of George VI, was invested as the twenty-first Prince of Wales in Caernarvon Castle – on the very day that a little girl, his future bride and *the ninth Princess of Wales*, celebrated her birthday in Norfolk: she was eight.

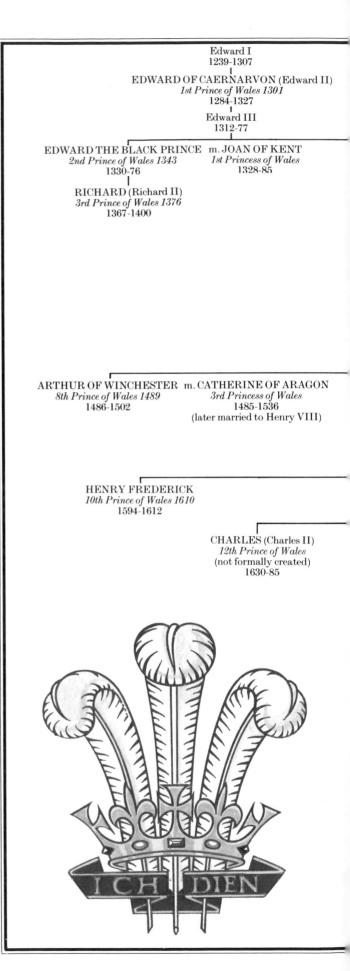

Edward I
1239-1307

EDWARD OF CAERNARVON (Edward II)
1st Prince of Wales 1301
1284-1327

Edward III
1312-77

EDWARD THE BLACK PRINCE
2nd Prince of Wales 1343
1330-76

m. JOAN OF KENT
1st Princess of Wales
1328-85

RICHARD (Richard II)
3rd Prince of Wales 1376
1367-1400

ARTHUR OF WINCHESTER
8th Prince of Wales 1489
1486-1502

m. CATHERINE OF ARAGON
3rd Princess of Wales
1485-1536
(later married to Henry VIII)

HENRY FREDERICK
10th Prince of Wales 1610
1594-1612

CHARLES (Charles II)
12th Prince of Wales
(not formally created)
1630-85

The Previous Princes and Princesses of Wales

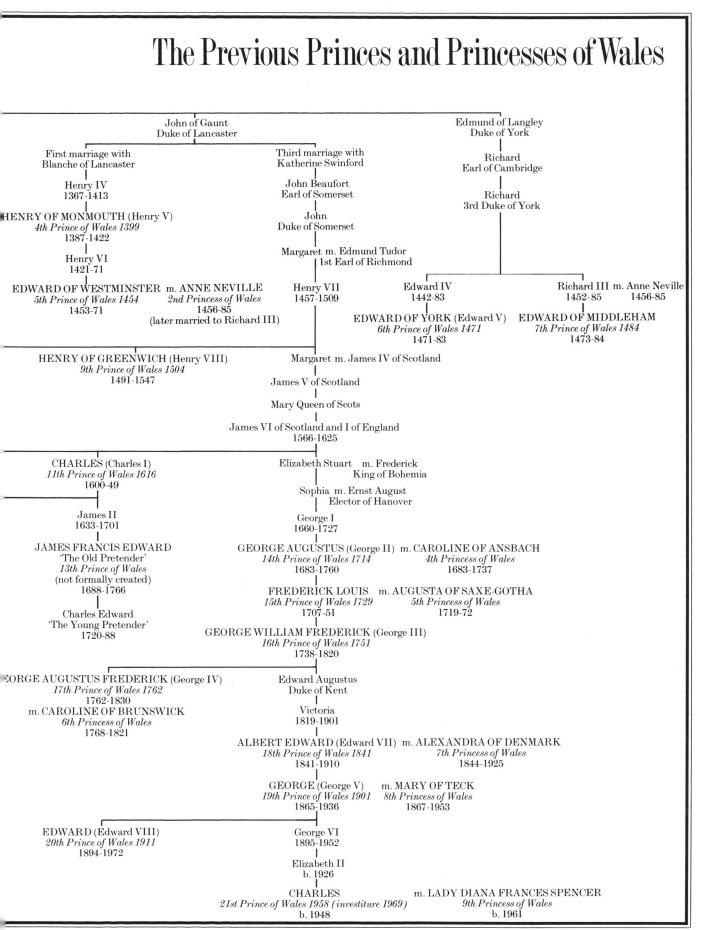

John of Gaunt
Duke of Lancaster

Edmund of Langley
Duke of York

First marriage with
Blanche of Lancaster

Third marriage with
Katherine Swinford

Richard
Earl of Cambridge

Henry IV
1367-1413

John Beaufort
Earl of Somerset

Richard
3rd Duke of York

HENRY OF MONMOUTH (Henry V)
4th Prince of Wales 1399
1387-1422

John
Duke of Somerset

Henry VI
1421-71

Margaret m. Edmund Tudor
1st Earl of Richmond

EDWARD OF WESTMINSTER   m. ANNE NEVILLE
5th Prince of Wales 1454   *2nd Princess of Wales*
1453-71   *1456-85*
(later married to Richard III)

Henry VII
1457-1509

Edward IV
1442-83

Richard III m. Anne Neville
1452-85   1456-85

EDWARD OF YORK (Edward V)
6th Prince of Wales 1471
1471-83

EDWARD OF MIDDLEHAM
7th Prince of Wales 1484
1473-84

HENRY OF GREENWICH (Henry VIII)
9th Prince of Wales 1504
1491-1547

Margaret m. James IV of Scotland

James V of Scotland

Mary Queen of Scots

James VI of Scotland and I of England
1566-1625

CHARLES (Charles I)
11th Prince of Wales 1616
1600-49

Elizabeth Stuart   m. Frederick
King of Bohemia

Sophia m. Ernst August
Elector of Hanover

James II
1633-1701

George I
1660-1727

JAMES FRANCIS EDWARD
'The Old Pretender'
13th Prince of Wales
(not formally created)
1688-1766

GEORGE AUGUSTUS (George II) m. CAROLINE OF ANSBACH
14th Prince of Wales 1714   *4th Princess of Wales*
1683-1760   *1683-1737*

FREDERICK LOUIS   m. AUGUSTA OF SAXE-GOTHA
15th Prince of Wales 1729   *5th Princess of Wales*
1707-51   *1719-72*

Charles Edward
'The Young Pretender'
1720-88

GEORGE WILLIAM FREDERICK (George III)
16th Prince of Wales 1751
1738-1820

GEORGE AUGUSTUS FREDERICK (George IV)
17th Prince of Wales 1762
1762-1830
m. CAROLINE OF BRUNSWICK
6th Princess of Wales
1768-1821

Edward Augustus
Duke of Kent

Victoria
1819-1901

ALBERT EDWARD (Edward VII) m. ALEXANDRA OF DENMARK
18th Prince of Wales 1841   *7th Princess of Wales*
1841-1910   *1844-1925*

GEORGE (George V)   m. MARY OF TECK
19th Prince of Wales 1901   *8th Princess of Wales*
1865-1936   *1867-1953*

EDWARD (Edward VIII)
20th Prince of Wales 1911
1894-1972

George VI
1895-1952

Elizabeth II
b. 1926

CHARLES
21st Prince of Wales 1958 (investiture 1969)
b. 1948

m. LADY DIANA FRANCES SPENCER
9th Princess of Wales
b. 1961

CHAPTER FIVE

Lady Diana

ON A WINDY JANUARY AFTERNOON ten weeks after the Welsh tour, the Prince and Princess of Wales visited the Dick Sheppard School on the outskirts of Brixton. The previous summer the area had been the scene of race riots. Now, outside the school, a sizeable police contingent looked nervous. They need not have worried. As the twenty-year-old Princess of Wales stepped out of the car the multi-racial crowd voiced their appreciation and welcome.

She had been married to the heir to the throne a mere six months. The crowd already felt, however, that she was *theirs*. A woman remarked, 'Fancy a girl so *young*, only just out of her teens, being so regal!'

That she certainly is now. But she has been in contact with royalty since her birth. For after all the speculations about a future wife for the Prince, the rumoured romances, the squiring of many girls, in the end he had finally chosen the girl literally from next door.

Lady Diana Frances Spencer was born on 1 July 1961 in Park House on the Sandringham estate, a few hundred yards from the royal family's own Norfolk country home. She was the third and youngest daughter of Edward John, Viscount Althorp (heir to the 7th Earl Spencer) and his wife, the Honourable Frances Ruth Burke Roche, youngest daughter of the 4th Baron Fermoy. There are many similarities between mother and daughter and an undeniably strong bond exists between them.

Johnnie, as her father was known, had been an equerry to the Queen; and two of Lady Diana's early and occasional playmates were Elizabeth II's younger

BELOW: *Lady Diana Spencer was born on 1 July 1961 in Park House, in the same bedroom in which her mother had been born in January 1936. The room is on the first floor to the right of the blue door. The family lived in Park House until Viscount Althorp became the 8th Earl Spencer in 1975.*
RIGHT: *The Princess of Wales had a happy and secure childhood at Park House, on the Sandringham estate.*

Viscount Althorp and the Honourable Frances Ruth Burke Roche married in Westminster Abbey in June 1954. A photograph of the bride's mother, Lady Fermoy, can be seen on the mantelpiece.

sons, Prince Andrew and Prince Edward. She was therefore accustomed to the presence of royalty from the start – although she never, as alleged, called the Queen 'Aunt Lillibet'. Her four grandparents had also been in the personal service of George VI and his Queen. She thus began life with distinct advantages.

The Althorps' fourth child (the third had died the day he was born) had the blessing of robust health as well as softly rounded, pretty features. At birth she weighed 7lbs 12ozs – 'a superb physical specimen,' as her father later observed. Her early years were happy, carefree and untroubled. All reports suggest she was easy-going, and although quite self-willed, always eager to please.

It was an almost idyllic existence in the seven-bed-roomed Victorian house, surrounded by a large garden, with a swimming-pool which was built in later years. She had two lively elder sisters, Sarah and Jane, a

younger brother, Charles (born in 1964), a nanny, a governess, two doting parents and a surfeit of pets, dogs, horses and hamsters. Not surprisingly, when Lady Diana became engaged, she could look back on those happy days of her childhood and remark, 'I feel my roots are in Norfolk. I have always loved it there.'

In many ways, however, it was a closeted, almost Edwardian upbringing. After all, this was the Sixties, the time of 'Swinging London', the Beatles, the Stones, pop music, drugs and an underground 'counter-culture'. But in Park House the Althorps' youngest daughter was being brought up to believe in the old-fashioned virtues of self-discipline, selflessness, good manners, service and duty.

It is almost as if she had been consciously trained for her future and demanding role as wife of the Prince of Wales. As her father so aptly said, 'The average family would not know what hit them if their daughter married the future King . . . But some of my family go back to the Saxons – so that sort of thing's not a bit new to me . . . Diana had to marry somebody, and I've known and worked for the Queen since Diana was a baby.' Or as she herself exclaimed, when asked if mixing with royalty would make her nervous, 'No, of course not! Why should it?'

From the age of four, in the tradition of continuity favoured by the aristocracy, she acquired a governess, Miss Gertrude Allen, who had looked after Lady Diana's mother when *she* was a child. Miss Allen, who died in 1981, taught the little girl to read and write: the stories she loved most were those about kings and queens, with happy endings. She was described by Miss Allen as a 'relaxed' girl and 'a tidy soul'.

Her father thought of her as 'sweet-natured' and 'practical'. Later he remembered her fondness for soft toys. 'She loved her soft toys, almost as much as she loved babies,' he said. 'She always loved babies.' She

In 1969 Lord and Lady Althorp were divorced; it was the year Lady Diana's paternal grandparents celebrated their golden wedding anniversary. Lady Diana (front left) is seen with (front row left to right) her younger brother Charles, and elder sisters, Sarah and Jane. Her father is seen in the back row (second from the right) standing next to his parents, the 7th Earl and Countess Spencer.

also adored her succession of furry pets: hamsters, jerbils and guinea-pigs, which were housed out in the stables at the back. Later she acquired a cat called Marmalade.

Until she was three, Lady Diana stayed in the nursery, but when her brother was born in 1964 – with a christening in Westminster Abbey and the Queen as a godparent – it was time to join her two sisters, Sarah and Jane, in the schoolroom next door to the dining-room. Miss Allen, known as 'Ally' to the children, later described Lady Diana as 'a conscientious girl. Not particularly bright . . . But she did *try*.'

For the next three years Lady Diana's life passed happily enough in the protected, privileged atmosphere of Park House – until her sixth birthday on 1 July 1967.

What happened next has often been misreported in recent years. The Althorps were divorced – but not in a sudden manner nor after Lady Althorp's 'desertion' of her children, an untruth that has pained her greatly and a deed she herself would deplore in another woman. In April 1982, to put the record straight and to protect her children by ending unjust and hurtful speculations,

she chose to make an exclusive statement for this book about what had been a very personal matter. Here is her own story.

'In the summer of 1967, Johnnie and I agreed to a trial separation. It was decided that I should take Diana and Charles with me to London, where they would both go to school in September – Sarah and Jane were already at boarding-school. A furnished house was rented in London and Diana, then aged six, and Charles, who was four, were enrolled at a girls' day school and a kindergarten respectively, both of which had been seen and approved by Johnnie. In early September I left Park House and drove to London. The following day, Diana, Charles and a nanny were put on a train by Johnnie and came to live with me. During the school term the two children returned to Park House most weekends to see their father, who in turn came to stay with us on his trips to London. In October I joined him and all four of our children, including Sarah and Jane, at Park House for the half-term holiday.

The whole family was reunited again at Christmas at Park House. It was my last Christmas there, for by now it had become apparent that the marriage had completely broken down. Johnnie now insisted that Diana and Charles should be sent to school in King's Lynn, not far from Park House, and that they should thenceforth stay at the house with him. He refused to let them return in the New Year to London. I strongly objected to this, and in a court action in June 1968 sought that the children be allowed to live with and be cared for by their mother. I lost the case and the custody of the children.'

Several factors worked against Lady Althorp – the weight of aristocratic opinion was against her, as was her own mother; and Norfolk, where the children had spent nearly all their lives, was a better place to bring them up than London. The law itself favoured the father, who happened to be the son and heir of an earl. Custody of children involved in a divorce case is invariably given to the mother, unless she is mentally deranged, a drug addict – or married to a nobleman. His rank and title give him prior claims.

In the meantime Lady Althorp, then aged thirty-one, had met Peter Shand Kydd, a 42-year-old married landowner with three children; and in April 1968, *before* her court action to keep her children, she was named in a divorce action brought by Janet Shand Kydd against her husband, Peter. The action was uncontested and Janet Shand Kydd was given custody of her children. Later that year, Lady Althorp began a divorce action against her husband, alleging cruelty. A counter-action was brought by him, alleging her adultery with Mr Shand Kydd, and a bitter court case followed. The

divorce went through in April 1969. On 2 May Lady Althorp and Peter Shand Kydd were married. They went to live for a time at Itchenor in Sussex. Robbed of a mother's role, though not of rights of access, she explained the situation to her children as objectively as she could and has remained on very good terms with all of them to this day.

At Park House, life without Lady Althorp continued; adjustments were made and au pairs were employed to look after the two younger children. Lady Diana, sent by her father to a day school, Silfield School in King's Lynn in 1968, remained there for over two years. During the holidays and at weekends she continued to see her mother, reacting to the divorce with the unthinking resilience of her age.

She was now acquiring a degree of self-confidence. Indeed at times she was quite assertive, beginning to show a more extrovert side to her character. She loved charades and dressing-up, revealing a sense of theatre and self-awareness which have subsequently stood her in such good stead. She also developed a talent for mimicry, which she could use to mischievous and telling effect.

An incident that ultimately had more effect on her than her parents' divorce occurred in these childhood years in Norfolk when she fell off a pony and broke her arm. It took three months to mend. As a result, and unusually for a girl of her background, she has little if any interest in horses and gave up riding altogether – although she said recently, 'I might take it up again . . . but very gently.' She has not done so as yet.

In 1970, when she was nine, her parents decided she should become a boarder at Riddlesworth Hall, a preparatory school near Diss in Norfolk. As she prepared to leave home, with her trunk labelled *D. Spencer*, her father took a photograph. It shows a sweet-faced girl with shoulder-length, corn-coloured hair, dressed in the school uniform of a dark red jacket and grey pleated skirt. It also shows the stamp of that beauty that would win so many hearts: the paradoxical, teasing combination of shyness and assurance, of reserve and a sunny, open nature.

Leaving home was as much of an upset as her mother's departure, especially for Lady Diana's father, who had become a sad and lonely figure, sometimes seen shopping for himself in King's Lynn. 'That was a dreadful day,' he has since admitted. 'Dreadful losing her.' Apparently she suffered from homesickness during her first weeks at boarding-school. But she soon settled down and began to enjoy herself.

Lady Diana spent part of her school holidays in Scotland with her mother, now married to Peter Shand Kydd. She is seen here in 1974 on the Isle of South Uist in the Outer Hebrides.

When Lady Diana was at Riddlesworth Hall she kept a guinea-pig which she called Peanuts.

The motto of Riddlesworth Hall is 'Facing Forward'. Despite this somewhat military Victorian ideal, the school's atmosphere was warm and friendly, providing a solid surrogate home, which was exactly what she needed as she entered her teens – especially as her holidays were now more sharply divided between her mother and father. This situation became even more complicated when the following year Mrs Shand Kydd moved to Scotland, to help her husband run a 1,000-acre hill-farm on the Isle of Seil near Oban in Argyll.

One of the agreeable features of Riddlesworth Hall was that the pupils were allowed to keep hamsters and guinea-pigs. Lady Diana's favourite was a guinea-pig called Peanuts, and during one holiday, at the Sandringham Show, she won First Prize in the Fur and Feather section for the obvious care she had lavished on Peanuts.

She was becoming a tall, strong, leggy girl and her prowess at swimming secured her a place in the school team. She was also keen on tennis – her mother had qualified for Junior Wimbledon in 1952. Albert Betts, who became the family butler after her parents' divorce, remembers her as developing into a 'self-reliant, loving, domesticated person. She washed and

ironed her own jeans, and did all her own chores. I was with the family when she was eleven to fifteen, and she was always immaculate.' He also remembers her sweet tooth: 'My wife [Elsie, the cook] used to make her a lot of raspberry and strawberry ice cream. Diana was very fond of lemon *soufflé* and loved chocolate cake with butter icing, which my wife used to make for her tuckbox before she went back to school.'

The school's headmistress, Miss Elizabeth Ridsdale – 'Riddy' to the girls – said later that the young Lady Diana was 'an extremely average' pupil. Miss Ridsdale recalled, 'She was always a decent, kind and happy little girl. Everyone seemed to like her . . . She was good at games, especially swimming. She took part in everything . . . What stands out in my mind is how awfully sweet she was with the little ones.' Like her future husband, she did not shine in the classroom. But ample demonstration was made of that virtue which is also conspicuously his: trying hard. Indeed at her next school she won an award 'For service'.

In 1973 she passed her Common Entrance exam, and went to West Heath, a small £3,000-a-year school near Sevenoaks, in Kent, where once again, although she failed to show any aptitude academically, everyone was impressed by her good humour, willingness to try, and above all her altruism. Once a week, Lady Diana used to visit an old lady in Sevenoaks, helping her with shopping and domestic chores; she also visited and assisted at a centre for handicapped children. Her headmistress, Miss Ruth Rudge, an Australian, said, 'She's a girl who notices what needs to be done and then does it willingly and cheerfully.'

While her classwork continued to be 'normal and average', Lady Diana, now a lofty teenager, began to broaden her outlook and win new friendships. It was at West Heath that she met Carolyn Pride, one of the three girls with whom she was later to share her London flat. Carolyn later summed up Lady Diana's qualities when she said, 'I love her sense of humour. I love her thoughtfulness and her kindness, and the fact that she's a very companionable person, someone with whom you could never be bored.'

She began to learn the piano, but soon gave it up. More important to her was dancing. Like many a schoolgirl she dreamed of becoming a prima ballerina. As she says, 'I am obsessed with ballet and I love tap-dancing. I always wanted to be a ballet dancer . . . But I just grew too tall.' Yet her height helped her with sport. Like Prince Charles, who had to follow the daunting example of his father's athletic excellence at Gordonstoun, Lady Diana was confronted with the fact that her mother, while at her school, Hatfield Heath, had been 'Captain of everything'. However, she herself won a dancing prize and several cups for swimming, diving and one for 'Service for the School'.

In the summer of 1975 there occurred an event that would considerably change her life. The 7th Earl Spencer died, and her father, Viscount Althorp, inherited the title, becoming the 8th Earl. Park House was abandoned and the new Earl Spencer moved up the M1 motorway to take over the family's ancestral seat, Althorp, a 450-year-old mansion near Northampton with an 8,488-acre estate. The following year he was named in divorce proceedings against Raine, the Countess of Dartmouth, initiated by her husband, the Earl of Dartmouth, and in July 1976 Earl Spencer wed the Countess at Caxton Hall Register Office in London. None of his four children attended the wedding – they were not told about it in advance.

The new Lady Spencer, a sparkling, do-gooding, go-getting personality and daughter of the prolific romantic novelist, Barbara Cartland, never succeeded

The present Earl and Countess Spencer outside Althorp, seat of the Spencer family. Sir John Spencer, great-great-grandfather of the first Lord Spencer, built the original Elizabethan house soon after 1508. It was not until 1786 that the 2nd Earl Spencer asked Henry Holland to remodel the house entirely – as we see it today.

in endearing herself to her stepchildren, who viewed her arrival with some animosity. Even today they have little affection for her. However, she soon set about reorganizing the rickety finances of Althorp and refurbishing its interior. And the following year she revealed her steely resourcefulness when Earl Spencer, at the age of fifty-five, suffered a massive brain haemorrhage. Doctors informed her that he stood only a 50 per cent chance of surviving. She determined to improve his chances, taking him from hospital to hospital, specialist to specialist, and finally she used her influence to obtain a 'miracle drug' for him, Azlocillin, available then in Germany but not in England. Her husband soon showed remarkable signs of recovery. Later he said, 'She saved my life. I love her dearly.'

Meanwhile, Lady Diana's schooldays were drawing to an early close. Her holidays at Althorp had not always been too agreeable under her stepmother's regime. But in her last month at West Heath she obtained leave to attend a weekend shooting party at home. The guest of honour was the Prince of Wales. She was introduced to him in a ploughed field by her sister, Lady Sarah. At that time she was sixteen and a half, he nearly twenty-nine. He thought her 'jolly'; she thought him 'pretty amazing'. Neither of them,

The Picture Gallery at Althorp houses one of the finest private collections in Europe. So much so that the 6th Earl Spencer, who found himself with far too many ancestral portraits, was persuaded in 1914 to sell some masterpieces to the art-dealer, Duveen, for export to America.

and certainly not Diana's schoolfriends, could ever have imagined that this meeting was the stuff of which journalists' dreams are made.

The following month, she left West Heath without taking any 'A' Levels, having decided not to try for them against her father's advice. Instead, on her mother's advice, she followed in the steps of her eldest sister, Lady Sarah, and went in January 1978 to a finishing school in Switzerland, the exclusive Institut Alpin Videmanette at Chateau d'Oex near Gstaad. But the routine of turning out 'well-bred' young ladies skilled in dressmaking, cooking, typing and speaking French, did not satisfy her. And she was homesick.

The headmistress, Madame Yersin, recalls, 'When Lady Diana arrived she was a lovely girl – but rather young for a sixteen-year-old . . . and while she was a

pretty girl, she was not the beauty she's blossomed into now.' Her French teacher had the impression of a rather more determined young lady. She said, 'Lady Diana was broad-minded, but she was also very idealistic about what she wanted for herself. She knew she wanted to work with children – and then she wanted to get married and have children of her own.' The future Princess of Wales spent only one term at the Institut. For some reason, she never settled down there.

On returning to England in March 1978, Lady Diana gravitated to London. But she did not, like so many girls with her background, pursue the pleasures of the debutante set. Her stepmother, Raine, had been 'Deb of the Year' in 1947. But Lady Diana was not attracted by such social frivolities: not for her a flashy night-life or fashionable parties. She wanted to be useful. For over a year, during which she passed her driving test, she looked after other peoples' babies and children as an unpaid nanny. During the summer she had worked for photographer, Jeremy Whitaker and his wife who live in Hampshire with their small daughter.

She also attempted to train as a ballet teacher at the Vacani School of Dancing in Brompton Road. 'She tried it for about a term,' said Betty Vacani, whose pupils over the years have included the Queen, Princess Margaret, Prince Charles, his sister and Prince Edward. 'But she realized that you've got to be absolutely dedicated, and she had rather a full social life. But the ballet helped her posture. She loved ballet . . . She was a rather shy, charming girl.'

Meanwhile, her father and mother clubbed together to buy her a flat in London, paying about £50,000 for a three-bedroomed flat at 60 Coleherne Court off the Old Brompton Road. Lady Diana moved in a few weeks after her eighteenth birthday in July 1979, and entered on the last part of her anonymous life.

She acquired three stalwart flatmates, who were to prove such loyal allies when Coleherne Court became one of the most famous addresses in England. First there was her schoolfriend, Carolyn Pride, who was studying music; she was soon followed by Anne Bolton and Virginia Pitman. It was an ideal set-up: a warm, convivial atmosphere for four like-minded girls, with few cares and few financial worries.

By September Lady Diana had a job: she began work at the Young England Kindergarten in Pimlico, run by Vicky Wilson and Kay Seth-Smith (now Mrs King), who had been to West Heath. The children, aged from two and a half to five, offspring of successful barristers, solicitors, merchant bankers, politicians and actors, included the great-grandson of the former Conservative Prime Minister, Mr Harold Macmillan. Employed as a part-time nursery assistant and called by the children, Miss Diana, for the first six months she worked for three afternoons a week. On the other two afternoons she looked after a little American boy, whom, she has said, 'was very special to me'. In the spring of 1980 she began working at the Kindergarten for three full days a week. Occasionally she cycled to work; on other days she drove her Volkswagen – until she crashed it. Her next car was a red Mini-Metro given to her by her father.

Young England is situated in a large, bright church hall with a blue-curtained stage at one end. Lady Diana relished her new role: it was what she had always wanted to do. Wearing a smock, she supervised the children's games and projects, helping them to draw and paint, build things with bricks, leggo and dough. On Mondays there were lessons in dancing and singing. There was movement and music on Tuesdays, with percussive band music and singing on Thursdays. Amid the cheerful noise of the kindergarten she concentrated on each child individually giving them her undivided attention. According to her mother, she was 'a pied-piper with children.'

LEFT: *Lady Diana learned to ski when she attended the Institut Alpin Videmanette, an exclusive finishing school in Switzerland near Gstaad.*
BELOW: *Lady Diana's three flatmates in the sitting-room of 60 Coleherne Court: (from left to right) Virginia Pitman, Carolyn Pride and Anne Bolton.*

The Young England Kindergarten in Pimlico run by Victoria Wilson (left) and Kay King (right). Lady Diana began working here in September 1979.

Back in the flat the atmosphere was homely, although sometimes chaotic. The hallway was cluttered with bicycles; in the sitting-room, where there was an upright piano, magazines were scattered around, including the satirical news magazine, *Private Eye*. A typical day in Lady Diana's life, according to a friend, was 'shopping at Harrods, perhaps for something for the flat. Or tea in Fortnum & Mason, before looking in the windows in Bond Street, or going for a wander among the fabrics in Liberty's.'

Virginia Pitman summed up her flatmate's lifestyle at this time as follows: 'She had a lot of friends; a few people came round to supper, that sort of thing, and she sometimes went to the ballet or the cinema and occasionally out to dinner, but she didn't go out a great deal at night. She liked to stay and relax at home and watch the telly and have a very quiet evening.' She also loved to dance. Virginia Pitman continued, 'We often came back and found her dancing round the flat, just on her own.' Her favourite pop-group at the time was Abba.

Then in August 1979 came an all-important invitation – to Balmoral. Lady Diana was asked to join the royal family as a guest of the Queen; she was just eighteen. She was invited as a companion for Prince Andrew, then nineteen. But though they became good friends, a possible romance between the good-looking Prince and the handsome girl never materialized, and the happy atmosphere was shattered when the family heard of Earl Mountbatten's assassination in Ireland. He was Prince Charles's favourite great-uncle.

In February 1980 she received another invitation, this time to Sandringham. The Prince of Wales, twelve years her senior, was there with his own friends and hardly spoke to her. But Prince Andrew had spoken approvingly of her to his elder brother, and three more royal invitations came her way that summer, after her nineteenth birthday. In July, Prince Charles asked her to a polo match, at Cowdray Park, where he was playing for *Les Diables Bleus*. A week later came another invitation, this time from Prince Philip to join the royal family on the Royal Yacht, *Britannia*, for Cowes Week. Finally, she was asked by the Queen to stay at Balmoral early in September for the Highland Games at Braemar. It was then that the royal romance had its real beginning.

But within a week it was no longer a family secret. A press photographer snapped Lady Diana watching the Prince salmon-fishing in the River Dee, and on Monday, 8 September, her name and face were blazoned in the newspapers for the first time.

A courtship that would have been irregular at the best of times, with the many widespread demands on Prince Charles's time, now had to steer a difficult course through scavenging packs of pressmen. It was more of an ordeal for her – he was used to it. But her skill in handling pushy children, and her sense of fun, came in very useful. She won her pursuers' respect, and more important, that of the Prince's family. She possessed natural qualities of tact, charm, good humour, strength of mind and fortitude that could well suit a future Queen of England.

Press harassment reached an intolerable pitch over Christmas and New Year. The Palace issued a statement, asking that the privacy of the royal family's holiday and home in Sandringham be observed – to

Lady Diana was a guest of the Queen at Balmoral in September 1980 when she was seen watching Prince Charles fishing. He is seen here, with his gun dog Harvey, returning from a fishing expedition.

little avail. Lady Diana herself continued to be the subject of unrelenting speculation, until *The Times* pulled off the scoop announcement that every newspaper had sought – of an engagement.

It was three weeks before this that the Prince proposed. On 5 February 1981 he dined with Lady Diana in his apartments at Buckingham Palace. As she was leaving the next day for a much-needed holiday in Australia with her mother and stepfather, Prince Charles advised her not to make up her mind immediately, but to give the matter some thought. However, she said 'Yes' on the spot. She later admitted, 'I never had any doubts about it.' Indeed, her down-to-earth realism was expressed the day the engagement was announced. After five hectic months of private uncertainty and public trial, she simply said, 'It wasn't a difficult decision in the end. It was what I wanted – it's what I want.'

The engagement announcement was made on Tuesday, 24 February 1981. The night before, Lady Diana had packed a suitcase at Coleherne Court: it was the end of her life as a private citizen. She got into her Mini-Metro and drove to Clarence House, where she would stay as the Queen Mother's guest for a few days. Afterwards she occupied a suite in Buckingham Palace.

The months leading up to the wedding were as hectic as those that had gone before, but for different reasons – she would soon be married and become the wife of a Prince and future King. Her manner and carriage became more confident, although there were sometimes tears – when she saw her fiancé leave Heathrow Airport for an official tour of New Zealand and Australia; and when the fixed stares of a crowd who surrounded her at a polo match just before the wedding were too much for her to bear.

There was also one more graceless press ordeal to endure. In Australia, Prince Charles had been telephoning her every day. Then a German magazine published what it claimed was a transcript of tapes recording the couple's conversations. The Prince's solicitors took out a High Court injunction to prevent the tapes being published in Britain. However, this proved to be unnecessary. The tapes were soon shown to be fakes. But the unpleasantness served as a reminder that in their hunger for 'news' some papers would stop at nothing.

Yet the press, by their fierce and daily concentration on her face and every move, ensured that her path towards the altar became a triumphal progress. The people began to adore her, and each appearance, when she ventured into the public's sight, was received with acclaim. The Girl Next Door had conquered not only the heir to the throne but his future subjects as well.

As the wedding day approached, universal interest rose to a high pitch of excitement. United by the media, the nation on the day reacted in a way seldom seen in peacetime, reminiscent of the joyfulness that greeted the Queen's Silver Jubilee celebrations in 1977. That Lady Diana's wedding could arouse a similar response was a splendid omen that one day she too would be a worthy Queen.

CHAPTER SIX

Homes for a Princess

HOME FOR THE PRINCESS until her engagement meant Park House and Althorp, the Isle of Seil and Coleherne Court. Now, at the age of twenty-one, she has two official homes of her own. Later she will inherit or be given other mansions, and as Queen will be mistress of more houses, castles and palaces than any woman in the world.

Lady Diana stayed at Clarence House, home of the Queen Mother, on her engagement to Prince Charles and also on the eve of her wedding. The original house was rebuilt by John Nash in 1825.

At present, of all the main royal residences, Clarence House – where she spent the first two nights of her engagement and the eve of her wedding – must have a special place in her affections. London home of the Queen Mother, whose considerable charm and good taste are reflected in the daintily eclectic decor and furnishings of the interior, this large and comfortable mansion overlooking The Mall was once an extension of St James's Palace. The two are still joined together and connected by a door. The house takes its name from a sea captain, William, Duke of Clarence (younger brother of George IV and later William IV), who was

*A bird's-eye view of Clarence House (centre) in 1858
before it was linked to St James's Palace (right) in 1873.
Lancaster House can be seen beyond the smaller façade
of Clarence House and Buckingham Palace is at the
top of The Mall. The scene shows the procession for
the wedding of the Princess Royal.*

its first royal occupant. Later occupants of Clarence
House included Queen Victoria's mother, the Duchess
of Kent; her second son Prince Alfred, Duke of Edinburgh; and her youngest son, the Duke of Connaught,
who died in 1942 during World War II.

In 1949, a young married couple moved into the
recently redecorated house – Princess Elizabeth and
the Duke of Edinburgh. With them came their baby
boy, Prince Charles, born the previous November. He
spent nearly three years of his childhood in Clarence
House, and Princess Anne was born there on 15 August
1950. But eighteen months later, on 6 February 1952,
George VI died and Princess Elizabeth suddenly
acceded to the throne. Her mother, the Queen Elizabeth, and her sister, Princess Margaret, moved into
Clarence House the following year, before the coronation of Elizabeth II on 2 June 1953.

The Queen Mother has now lived at Clarence House
for over twenty-eight years. The Royal Lodge, in
Windsor Great Park, renovated and used by George IV
when he was Prince Regent, has been her country
home in England for fifty years. She also has two
Scottish homes: Birkhall, on the Balmoral estate, and
the Castle of Mey, six miles from John o' Groats. In
time, some or all of these homes may be inherited by her
grandchildren. One at least will become the additional
home of her eldest grandson and his wife.

The Prince and Princess of Wales at present have
two official homes, although apartments will continue
to be maintained for them in Buckingham Palace,
Windsor Castle, Balmoral Castle and Sandringham;
and if they choose they can stay at lesser royal residences, such as Craigowan and Delnadamph, two
lodges on the Balmoral estate, and at the six-bed-
roomed Wood Farm near Sandringham. These smaller,
agreeable country homes, far more manageable to run
than castles and palaces, are used as weekend retreats
by the Queen and her family, whose natural inclinations
are to live simply and not in regal splendour.

Prince Charles, as Duke of Cornwall, can also
stay on properties owned and managed by the Duchy

of Cornwall, whose possessions amount to 129,000 acres, mainly in the West Country. He has lodged more than once at the Home Farm, Stoke Climsland, Cornwall, and he has a cottage called Tamarisk on St Mary's in the Isles of Scilly. The cottage is also used as a holiday home by the families of Prince Michael of Kent and of the young Duke of Gloucester.

In London, the official residence of the Prince and Princess is in the northwest part of Kensington Palace, overlooking Kensington Green, in what are known as Apartments 8 and 9. Their neighbours at No. 10 are Prince and Princess Michael of Kent. Apartment 8 was previously occupied for nearly fifty years by the Dowager Countess of Granville, until 1938. During World War II, in October 1941, Apartments 8 and 9 were badly damaged by incendiary bombs and remained burned-out and derelict for more than a generation, until 1975, when a costly programme of repair and restoration was begun by the Department of the Environment. In 1981 structural alterations and some further redecoration of the rooms took place when it was known who the next occupants would be. It was hoped that the royal couple would be able to move in before the end of that year. But it was not until 14 May 1982 that they spent their first night there. Until then,

ABOVE: *Birkhall, the Queen Mother's eighteenth-century Deeside home, was originally purchased for the future Edward VIII in 1852.*
BELOW: *Tamarisk, the four-bedroomed cottage belonging to Prince Charles as Duke of Cornwall on St Mary's in the Isles of Scilly, off Land's End, Cornwall.*

Prince Charles and his wife keep a set of rooms in Windsor Castle – the largest castle in England.

Sandringham in Norfolk, the county where the Princess spent her childhood, is a favourite home of the couple.

the Prince's suite of rooms on the second floor of Buckingham Palace was extended to include accommodation for the Princess and her staff.

The Prince and Princess of Wales live in Kensington Palace in London. Their apartments are situated on the left behind the wall that borders Kensington Green.

The various buildings around the three courtyards that now comprise Kensington Palace had their genesis in a small country house built *circa* 1605. It passed through various hands until, as Nottingham House, it was sold by the Earl of Nottingham in 1689 to William III. He bought it for 18,000 guineas on the persuasion of his Queen, Mary II, and chiefly for health

The new porch at the entrance to Apartment 8 which leads into a hall and a staircase that joins the main Georgian staircase connecting both apartments.

reasons – their low-lying London residence, the Palace of Whitehall by the River Thames, was subject to miasmic mists and damps, which aggravated King William's asthma. Nottingham House was virtually rebuilt and greatly enlarged by Sir Christopher Wren. Mary II died of smallpox in her bedchamber in the new Palace in December 1694. Her husband died there too, in March 1702.

Queen Anne and her husband also died in the Palace, she in 1714. Her successor, George I, initiated another phase of substantial rebuilding, the new rooms (now State Apartments open to the public) being decorated by William Kent. He also decorated the apartments erected on the north side of Green Cloth Court, where the King's German mistress, the Duchess of Kendal, was installed. The courtyard, with cloisters arcaded by square pillars of brick and brightened by tubs of geraniums, took its name from the Board of Green Cloth, the accounting and judicial sections of the royal household, which had previously occupied the buildings there. It was later named Prince of Wales's Court, probably after the cello-playing and sporty eldest son of George II, Prince Frederick. His sisters gave their title to Princesses' Court, previously known as Pump

Court. South of these two courtyards is the third and largest, called Clock Court.

George II and his wife, Queen Caroline, improved the gardens and grounds of the Palace, creating the Round Pond and the Serpentine. George II died in Kensington Palace in October 1760, many years after his Queen. His mistresses, even in the Queen's life-time, also lived in the Palace in Prince of Wales' Court.

Young George III made homes for himself and his Queen elsewhere, rebuilding and extending Buckingham House and Windsor Castle. Some of their thirteen surviving children found homes, however, in Kensington Palace, including their fourth son, the Duke of Kent; their sixth son, the Duke of Sussex; and their scandalous daughter-in-law, Caroline, Princess of Wales. She lived in the Palace from 1807 to 1814. Five years later, the only daughter of the middle-aged Duke of Kent and his corpulent German wife was born in the east wing of Clock Court. She was christened Princess Victoria in the Cupola Room on 24 June 1819. Her father died eight months later.

Constantly supervised by her mother and the Duchess's crooked Comptroller, Princess Victoria grew up in Kensington Palace in what are now the State Apartments, sleeping in the same bed as her mother. At dawn on 20 June 1837 the Duchess, aroused by the arrival of important visitors, the Archbishop of Canterbury and the Lord Chamberlain, Lord Conyngham, woke 'the dear Child with a kiss'. The young Princess wrote in her diary: 'I got out of bed and went into the sitting-room (only in my dressing-gown and *alone*) and saw them. Lord Conyngham then acquainted me that my poor uncle, the King, was no more and had expired at 12 minutes past 2 this morning and consequently that I am *Queen*.' She was barely eighteen. One of her first acts was to provide herself with a bedroom and a single bed in which she slept that night for the first time on her own. A few weeks later the teenage Queen and remain so for life.

Nearly fifty years later another baby was born in the room in which Queen Victoria had slept with her mother. In May 1867 the Duchess of Teck gave birth to Victoria Mary, who in time became Princess of Wales and the Queen of King George V.

Queen Victoria was the last British monarch to live in Kensington Palace, although two of her daughters had homes there. Her final visit to the Palace took place on 15 May 1899, just before her eightieth birthday. She was carried in a chair up to the first floor to view the State Apartments, which were about to be opened to the public. When her grand-daughter, Princess Alice of Athlone, died in January 1981, aged ninety-seven, after living in her Clock House apartments for fifty-eight years, the last surviving link with Queen Victoria's reign came to an end.

Other apartments in Clock Court have been occupied by Princess Marina, Duchess of Kent, who died in 1968, and by the widowed Princess Alice, Duchess of Gloucester, who still lives there – as does Princess Margaret and her son and daughter at No. 1a Clock Court. Prince Charles used to refer to the Palace as 'the ants' nest' because of the four royal aunts who lived there. Now it has younger tenants, and houses the London apartments of the Duke and Duchess of Gloucester; of the younger son of Princess Marina, Prince Michael of Kent, his wife and their two children; and of Princess Alexandra and her husband and family. Opposite the west wing of the Palace, in the Old Barracks, live Lady Jane Fellowes and her husband, Robert Fellowes, who is Assistant Private Secretary to the Queen.

Apartments 8 and 9, now the London home of the Prince and Princess of Wales, take up the three storeys of the house in Prince of Wales's Court that was once occupied by mistresses of George I and George II. The apartments, connected by the four flights of a fine

---

Highgrove House is set in a small park at Doughton, near Tetbury in Gloucestershire – the whole estate consists of 348 acres of land.

Georgian staircase that largely survived bombing in the war, have been newly decorated by a 52-year-old South African interior designer, Dudley Poplak. They consist of a double drawing-room with flock wallpaper, a sitting-room for the Princess, a study for the Prince, a dining-room, a master-bedroom suite with a new bathroom, marbled and mirrored, two guest bedrooms, a nursery suite, several bathrooms, a breakfast room with an adjoining music room, and rooms for staff. These latter are divided between offices on the ground floor and bedrooms in the dormer-windowed attics. There is also a barbecue pit on the roof and a helicopter pad not far from the apartments. Ample as the apartments are they are not big enough to accommodate the family of four children that the couple are expected to have.

The same can be said of Highgrove, their country home in Gloucestershire. Indeed, if the Princess has four children within the next ten years, it seems likely that both Highgrove and the apartments in Kensington Palace will have to be given up in favour of larger establishments.

The freehold of Highgrove House and its 348 acres (almost the size of Hyde Park) was bought by Prince Charles through the Duchy of Cornwall in 1980 for about £800,000: the price included several cottages,

The gardens at Highgrove before they were landscaped by Lanning Roper, an American architect who trained as a landscape-gardener in Britain.

stables, a dairy and some barns. A mile southwest of the charming South Cotswold market town of Tetbury, the house is set in a neat little park by the A433 and the hamlet of Doughton, pronounced 'Duffton'. Humberts, the estate agents, who sold the property to the Prince, described it in their brochure as 'a distinguished Georgian house with spacious but easily managed accommodation comprising 4 Reception Rooms, Domestic Quarters, 9 Bedrooms (5 with Dressing Room), 6 Bathrooms, Nursery Wing, full central heating.' A pleasant enough grey stone building, facing northeast, and adorned at the rear with magnolia and wisteria, the house was distinguished, however, by its lack of distinction until now.

Highgrove was built between 1796 and 1798 by a young advocate, John Paul Paul, whose original name was Tippetts. His father, Josiah Tippetts, changed his

surname to Paul in 1789 when he inherited the lands of his uncle, John Paul of Tetbury. Young John Paul Paul built his house on land which he had inherited from his maternal grandfather, Robert Clark. A local worthy, J.P. Paul became High Sheriff of Wiltshire in 1807 when he was thirty-five; in 1818 he bought the manor of Doughton. Upon his death, Highgrove passed to his second son, Walter Paul, who in 1860 sold his estates to a Colonel Stracey. He in turn sold them a few years later to a Warwickshire barrister, William Yatman.

In 1891 the spire and tower of Tetbury's parish church, which had become unstable and dangerous, were dismantled and rebuilt. Mr Yatman paid for the reconstruction, which cost £10,000, as a memorial to his deceased son, a captain in the 3rd Dragoon Guards. He liked to see the spire from the front windows of Highgrove and kept the view clear of trees. The work was completed in 1893, when the house was badly damaged in a fire, two years before the birth of George VI.

Soon afterwards Mr Yatman sold Highgrove to a Captain Mitchell. He rebuilt and restored the house, and after his death his widow remained there until 1945. while her stepson, Lieutenant-Colonel Mitchell, occupied the manor of Doughton. The next owner of Highgrove was Lieutenant-Colonel Morgan-Jones of the Life Guards, who enlarged the estate. When he died in 1964 the house and grounds were bought by Conservative M.P., the Right Honourable Maurice Macmillan, son of the former Prime Minister, Harold Macmillan. Seldom resident at Highgrove, he used to let the house, and for two years it was occupied by James Roosevelt, a retired American general and son of the former American President, Franklin D. Roosevelt.

Both the Prince and Princess of Wales are distantly related to previous occupants of the house, including the man who built it. The Princess is linked genealogically with the Roosevelts through her American maternal great-grandmother, Frances Work, a New

Much work has been done on refurbishing Highgrove. Real oak kitchen furniture similar to the range of units shown here has been fitted in the new kitchen.

York heiress, who could claim family connections with no less than eight American presidents. Prince Charles is himself connected through the Queen Mother to John Paul Paul, with whom he has a common sixteenth-century ancestor in Richard Pitt of Weymouth.

Mr Macmillan put Highgrove up for sale in the spring of 1980. Princess Anne, by then living with her husband at Gatcombe Park eight miles away – she had once considered buying Highgrove herself – telephoned her eldest brother and told him the house was on the market. He saw it and bought it in the late summer.

Work on the house began slowly, until Prince Charles and Lady Diana became engaged – after which various costly renovations proceeded apace – most significantly the construction (it is said) of a steel-walled room within the house to protect the family from any kind of attack. Lady Diana involved herself in the more aesthetic aspects of redecoration, adding her own ideas about decor and furnishing – already illustrated in her flat in Coleherne Court, where she had painted the sitting-room walls primrose yellow and

Hector Cole, a wrought-iron craftsman from Great Somerford in Wiltshire, made the new gates for Highgrove. He is seen here at work on the gates with his design in the background. The gates were hung in March 1982.

decorated the bathroom with wallpaper covered in red cherries. At Highgrove she has communicated her preferences not just to the Prince but to the interior designer, Dudley Poplak. The hall is rag-rolled in pink, the green drawing-room has attractive fringed curtains, and there are many polished wood floors in the house.

With a face-lift inside and out the old building has been much improved and brightened. The kitchen and butler's pantry have been completely re-equipped with a set of some one hundred units worth £10,000 – the gift of a West Midlands firm, the Landywood Cabinet Company. A cottage on the estate was fitted with another expensive gift of kitchen units. But the kitchen units in the apartments at Kensington Palace were bought and paid for by the couple.

A gift of nursery furniture worth £1,200 (including a four-poster cot) was returned to the donors, a North London baby shop, when the Palace heard that a similar cot was being offered as a prize in a newspaper competition. The Princess then bought furnishings and

furniture for the nursery worth £400 from Dragons, a baby boutique in Knightsbridge.

The windows of Highgrove, equipped with bullet-proof glass, gaze out on lawns and gardens landscaped by Lanning Roper. A swimming-pool, presented by the Army, has not yet been installed. But at the end of the curved drive stands a new set of ironwork gates, a wedding present from the people of Tetbury.

Altogether, Highgrove is now a very desirable and well-fortified residence. It is also well-situated, and provides a good base for the Prince's social and sporting activities. London is 100 miles away along the M4 motorway; the Principality of Wales is less than thirty miles away across the Severn Bridge; and most of the Duchy of Cornwall's estates are a two-hour drive away or less. Moreover, Princess Anne and her husband are neighbours – as are Prince and Princess Michael of Kent, who live in the delightful Nether Lypiatt Manor near Stroud – and several good friends of the Prince live within fifty miles of the house. His many sporting interests are well catered for locally, with polo in Cirencester Park, racing at Cheltenham, Bath, Chepstow and Newbury, and hunting with the Beaufort Hunt centred at nearby Badminton House. Highgrove, within Beaufort Hunt country, has hunt-jumps in

Princess Anne and Captain Mark Phillips bought Gatcombe Park at Minchinhampton in Gloucestershire from the late Lord Butler of Saffron Walden in 1976. The house, built in 1770, has fine landscaped grounds and 1,263 acres of estate.

most of its fields, which are at present largely put down to grass.

None the less, the house itself is but a hundred yards from a main road, the A433 and a Public Footpath, and despite rows of newly planted young sycamore trees, the front of the house can be seen by anyone passing along the road towards Bath or from the footpath. At night, car headlights must be visible in turn from the windows. Public rights of way virtually surround the house. It is probably the least private of all royal residences, as well as of the least architectural merit, and for the police it is a security nightmare. The grounds and nearby roads are continually patrolled and under constant surveillance.

As the couple's household and staff are few in number, they can be accommodated comfortably in the house. However, any extra staff and bodyguards required for major social occasions have to be lodged elsewhere in estate cottages or in a local inn, the White Hart in Tetbury.

The choice of Highgrove as a royal family home seems in several respects to have been ill-considered. It is not as secluded, as commodious, as attractive, as satisfactory, as suitable and as befitting a prince as it might have been – as some of the country houses in the neighbourhood and many elsewhere are. A house and a home like Althorp would have been ideal. But perhaps the Prince of Wales will one day *build* a new home for his Princess, as Queen Victoria's eldest son did at Sandringham one hundred years ago.

CHAPTER SEVEN

Household Matters

ALTHOUGH THE PRINCESS is the daughter of an earl, she was not brought up with a plethora of servants to wait on her, like those that attended on her Sandringham neighbour, the Queen – although her father had an indoor and outdoor staff. At Park House when she was very young she had a nanny, Judith Parnell,

The Princess of Wales' family has been in the personal service of the royal family since the reign of George IV. Her grandmother, Ruth, Lady Fermoy, is a Woman of the Bedchamber to the Queen Mother and the two grandmothers are close friends.

and then a governess. After her mother and father separated in 1967, an au pair was engaged by him to look after his four children when they were not at school. It was not until the summer of 1975, when her father became the 8th Earl Spencer and moved into Althorp, that his teenage daughter went for the first time, and not as a guest, to live in a stately home which maintained a full staff of servants.

She had been a visitor there before, when her grandfather was the Earl, but not very often. None the less, because of her aristocratic friends and background, she was used to the presence of servants, and despite

The Princess of Wales acquired her first attendants when she became engaged to Prince Charles. She is seen here on 22 May 1981 in Tetbury with four of her bodyguards. Her red and white silk outfit was designed by Jasper Conran and her shoes by Rayne.

their absence in London when she lived at Coleherne Court, she had become accustomed to the ubiquitous attentions of the Queen's household and staff when she was a guest at Sandringham and Balmoral.

Service of a more exalted sort was of course nothing new to her. All four of her grandparents, the Spencers and Fermoys, as well as four great-aunts, had been in the personal service of George VI and his Queen. In the 1950s her father had been equerry to both George VI and his daughter, Elizabeth II. The Princess's grandmother, Ruth, Lady Fermoy, has been a Woman of the Bedchamber to the Queen Mother, Prince Charles's grandmother, for twenty-five years. The two ladies are close and dear friends, as were their husbands, and over the last few years they have viewed the growing association of their grandchildren with fond delight and their alliance with the greatest pleasure.

The Princess acquired her first royal attendant on the morning of Wednesday, 25 February 1981, the day after her engagement was announced. He was Chief Inspector Paul Officer, one of the three Special Branch police officers assigned to protect the Prince and now his fiancée.

The other two police officers responsible for her safety, then and now, are Superintendent John Maclean and Detective Inspector Jim McMaster. Maclean, a sturdy Scot, has been with the Prince for many years and inevitably, seeing so much of him, has become a firm friend. These two have been joined since the engagement by Colin Trimming, called 'Shoestring' by the press, and Graham Smith; both are detective inspectors. Colin Trimming previously worked for Princess Anne. Detective Inspector Alan Peters, who had worked part-time as a bodyguard in 1981, was promoted to full-time protector when in March 1982, Detective Inspector David Robinson was 'moved on' after six months with the Princess – apparently he was overtly tense and jumpy on her informal excursions and shopping trips.

Paul Officer left the Prince's service some months after the engagement to become a superintendent. It was rumoured afterwards that the Prince's fiancée had not been particularly taken with Officer and that this hastened his departure. Usually, however, when a

Ken Stronach, valet to Prince Charles, collects Prince Charles's hand luggage at Delhi during his trip to India at the end of 1980.

wife moves into a bachelor establishment, some domestic changes are made. As it is, her arrival is also said to have caused the resignation of Stephen Barry, one of the Prince's two valets. The other valet, Ken Stronach, was once employed in the service of the late Earl Mountbatten.

Barry, a 32-year-old bachelor, had looked after Prince Charles for more than twelve years. Latterly he had begun attending some rather flamboyant publicity functions and attracted overmuch press attention by his gaily indifferent choice of companions. But a clash of personalities seems to have been mainly responsible for his departure – the valet disagreeing with the Princess about her husband's clothes. He was also reluctant, it seems, to work at Highgrove – 'far from the London scene'. Barry, who was paid about £6,500 a year – and whose perks included a clothing allowance, the use of Palace cars and a flat in Kennington – left the Prince's service in April 1982. He was replaced by Paul Chant, aged thirty-two, and previously a Corporal of Horse in the Household Cavalry.

The Prince's official household, as distinct from his police bodyguards and staff, numbers six. Chief of it is his private secretary, the Honourable Edward Adeane, a former libel lawyer, aged forty-two, who receives about £20,000 a year. His father, Sir Michael, now Lord Adeane, was a long-serving Private Secretary to the Queen. Francis Cornish, the Prince's Assistant Private Secretary, is forty and is on secondment from the Foreign Office who pay his salary of about £18,000 a year. His secretary and accountant is Michael Colborne, who was a Fleet Chief Petty Officer with the Royal Navy on HMS *Norfolk* when he was asked by the Prince to join his household. Major John Winter, of the Parachute Regiment, who receives about £13,000 a year, paid by the Army, is the Prince's Equerry. His Extra Equerry is Squadron Leader Sir David Checketts, who served the Prince for nine years as his Private Secretary while the Prince was at Timbertop and Cambridge. Captain Robert Mason of the Welsh Guards fills in as Temporary Equerry when required.

The first full-time member of the Princess's household to be appointed – at £16,000 a year – was Oliver Everett. Aged thirty-nine, married with four children, he was recalled from diplomatic service at the British Embassy in Madrid to supervise the correspondence

after the engagement was announced and to deal with the Princess's social and official requirements. Formerly an Assistant Private Secretary to the Prince, until he was replaced by Francis Cornish, Oliver Everett became Private Secretary to the Princess on 31 July 1981 as well as Comptroller to both her and the Prince. Another initially unofficial appointment was that of Evelyn Dagley as the Princess's lady's maid. Miss Dagley, in her late twenties, had previously been employed by the royal family as a housemaid in Burkingham Palace.

ABOVE LEFT: *The Honourable Edward Adeane (centre), Private Secretary to the Prince of Wales, with the Prince on a visit to the headquarters of the Parachute Regiment Brigade at Fatehpur Sikri, India.*
ABOVE RIGHT: *Oliver Everett became Private Secretary to the Princess of Wales on 31 July 1981. He is seen here walking beside the Princess (to the left), with Hazel West, lady-in-waiting, following behind, during a visit to Bridgend in South Wales on 7 April 1982.*
BELOW: *Anne Beckwith-Smith is the only full-time lady-in-waiting to the Princess of Wales. Her first public appearance was on the tour of Wales in October 1981.*

It was not until 25 September 1981 that the names of the Princess's three ladies-in-waiting were announced. Until then she had been accompanied on official outings and engagements by her sisters and women-friends. The ladies-in-waiting, all carefully chosen and personally asked by the Princess if they would accept their appointments, were advised about their future roles by, among others, Lady Susan Hussey, one of the Queen's long-serving and loyal Women of the Bedchamber.

All three are somewhat older than the Princess, the youngest and only full-time lady-in-waiting being Miss Anne Beckwith-Smith, aged thirty. She is the daughter of Major Peter Beckwith-Smith, who is Clerk of the Course at Epsom and at Sandown Park during the flat season; she was educated at Southover Manor, West Heath and Queensgate. After studying History of Art in Florence and in Paris, she worked for nearly three years at the Arts Council, helping to organize exhibitions. Before her appointment as lady-in-waiting she worked in the English Picture Department at Sotheby's for four years.

Lavinia Baring, aged thirty-one, daughter of Sir Mark and Lady Baring, is married to her second cousin, the Honourable Vivian Baring, second son of the 3rd Earl of Cromer. Sir Mark, a grandson of the 1st Earl of Cromer, has been General Commissioner for Income Tax since 1966. Mrs Baring has two sons and lives near

Lavinia Baring, wife of the Honourable Vivian Baring, acts as a part-time lady-in-waiting. She accompanied the Princess of Wales to Northampton, when the Princess opened the new Head Post Office on 20 November 1981.

Westerham in Kent. She was educated at Heathfield, studied at Queen's Secretarial College in London, and after that worked for a time for the Winston Churchill Memorial Trust.

The eldest of the extra ladies-in-waiting is 38-year-old Hazel West, wife of Lieutenant-Colonel George West of the Grenadier Guards; he retired from the Army in 1980 and has been Assistant Comptroller of the Lord Chamberlain's Office in Buckingham Palace since 1981. Mrs West is the youngest daughter of the late Lieutenant-Colonel Sir Thomas Cook (M.P. and a Commissioner of St John's Ambulance Brigade) and Lady Cook of Norfolk. She was educated in England and Paris and studied music and cooking.

Lavinia Baring and Hazel West, acting as companions more than personal assistants, are generally employed about once a month, more so during the summer. Their only payment consists of expenses, although there are perks associated with each occasion they attend. Anne Beckwith-Smith, based at Buckingham Palace, is the Princess's chief personal assistant and secretary, as well as her principal companion.

Although the ladies-in-waiting share the Princess's public life and engagements, not all such occasions are spectacular or glamorous and they are required to do much standing about, looking elegant but not obtrusive. Stamina is a prerequisite, as are comfortable shoes – so too are tact, commonsense, quick-thinking and a sense of humour. On duty their handbags are packed with emergency sewing materials, tissues, cosmetics, headache pills, a nail-file, mirror and spare tights. They must carry the many bouquets and gifts presented to the Princess. Often it will seem tiring and trying. But they will become close friends of a future Queen and remain so for life.

Anne Beckwith-Smith and Evelyn Dagley both see more of the Princess than any other person, travelling with her wherever she goes.

At Highgrove, the third most important member of her staff is cook-housekeeper, Rosanna Lloyd. Aged thirty-five, the unmarried daughter of a Welsh solicitor, she took up her duties in January 1982. Before that the occasional Palace cook lent a hand in Highgrove's kitchen. At other times, a superior 'meals-on-wheels' service run locally by Bridget Parke was employed. In her fifties, Miss Parke used to cook regularly for Prince Charles when, as a bachelor, he bought and first moved into Highgrove. Rosie Lloyd, who previously cooked at the Wolf's Castle Hotel near Haverfordwest, is not normally expected to produce anything too exotic: the Prince's preference is for simple English fare, like scrambled eggs with smoked salmon on toast. But she has a wide range of recipes: from bread and butter pudding, to venison in beer with chestnuts, and *coulibiac*, a Russian fish pie. Borsch will certainly be

ABOVE LEFT: *Hazel West, wife of Lieutenant-Colonel George West, is the eldest of the ladies-in-waiting. She is seen here at her home in Warwickshire.*
ABOVE RIGHT: *Barbara Barnes with May and Amy Tennant whom she cared for before her royal appointment.*

on some menus: the Princess once submitted a recipe for borsch to a charity cookbook as one of her favourite dishes. She is also said to like lemon *soufflé*, chocolate cake with butter icing, hamburgers, and homemade fudge. She has a sweet tooth and loves sweets.

The Kensington Palace apartments have their own cook-housekeeper, and the couple's establishments in London and Gloucestershire each have a small permanent staff, with a butler, two or three maids and as many footmen. Any additional staff, required for large dinner parties, is borrowed for the occasion from Buckingham Palace.

The couple's butler at Kensington Palace, Alan Fisher, was employed by the Duke and Duchess of Windsor between 1954 and 1960, and after that he worked in America for Bing Crosby and his family for over sixteen years. Mr Fisher, who lives in with his wife,

has said of his previous employers, 'The Duchess taught me everything I know – twice over. She has impeccable taste . . . Whether I am fit to work for anyone after Mrs Crosby remains to be seen . . . She spoiled me.'

The appointment of Barbara Barnes as the royal baby's nanny was officially confirmed on 10 May 1982. Miss Barnes, aged thirty-nine, unmarried and the daughter of a retired Norfolk forestry worker, has had no formal training and does not wear a uniform. She was previously employed by the Honourable Colin Tennant and his wife, Lady Anne, both close friends of Princess Margaret (Lady Anne is a lady-in-waiting to her) and has looked after three of the Tennants' five children, Christopher, now aged fourteen, and his twin sisters, Amy and May, aged eleven. Lady Anne has said of her former nanny, 'She is exceptionally firm, with a great sense of humour. The children absolutely adore her.' 'I don't see any different problems,' said Miss Barnes, 'in bringing up a royal baby. I treat all children as individuals.' She has a good singing voice, believes in children having fun and lots of fresh air, and hopes the Princess will be much involved in the bringing-up of her first child.

CHAPTER EIGHT

Wedding Presents

Highgrove and the Kensington Palace apartments will be furnished largely from the thousands of wedding presents the couple received. Just over one thousand of these presents – a tenth of the ten thousand and more that were received before the wedding and for six months after it – were on display in St James's Palace from 5 August until 4 October 1981. The exhibition, which included the wedding dress, attracted over 207,000 people. They cheerfully queued for hours every day in all weathers – sometimes the orderly queue stretched for one-and-a-half miles. After costs and overheads had been met, the London exhibition raised £85,000 for charities concerned with the disabled.

The wedding dress had pride of place, standing in a Harrods' show-case at the end of the Palace's Picture Gallery. The bouquet was a confection of silk flowers made by Longman's, the florists, a clever copy of the original bouquet of golden roses, gardenias, stephanotis, orchids, lilies of the valley, freesias, myrtle and veronica, that had been created by the Worshipful Company of Gardeners. On either side of The Dress the page-boy uniform, worn originally by Edward van Cutsem, and the dress of the smallest bridesmaid, Clementine Hambro, were exhibited.

Barkers of Kensington arranged the presents in their show-cases – the most opulent, from heads of state and foreign royalty, being separated from the rest and assembled in the Throne Room. Arab monarchies gave the most costly gifts: a gold choker studded with gems from the Crown Prince and Princess of Jordan; two Patek Philippe sets of watches and rings made from onyx, diamonds, coral and gold from the Emir and Heir Apparent of Qatar, with corresponding cufflinks, necklace and earrings; a two-foot-long solid gold dhow from the Amir of Bahrain; and a magnificent set of sapphire and diamond jewelry from the Crown Prince of Saudi Arabia, who also provided a malachite box, encrusted with gems and gold, in which to store the jewelry. His gift, believed to be worth £250,000, makes it seem possible that the thousand presents on display were worth well over £1 million. If this is so, the ten thousand presents received by the couple could have been worth as much as £10 million.

Not all, however, were purchased by the donors at the full retail price: firms and shops give royalty and presidents discounts. American newspapers claimed that the gift of the President of the United States, a

The Princess of Wales' wedding dress was exhibited with her attendants' costumes. The dress, designed by David and Elizabeth Emanuel, was made of ivory silk taffeta. The bodice had antique lace panels and, like the tulle veil, was embroidered with mother-of-pearl sequins. A tiny gold horseshoe was also added for luck. The veil was held in place by the Spencer family tiara. The sweeping 25-foot detachable train was trimmed and edged with lace.

ABOVE: *Their Royal Highnesses the Crown Prince and Princess of Jordan presented the royal couple with a fabulous gold choker studded with gems.*
RIGHT: *A glass bowl and malachite base were sent by the President of the United States of America and his wife, Mrs Reagan.*

large engraved glass bowl, was especially reduced for Mrs Reagan from £40,000 to £4,000. Three large vases came from Mauritius, Korea and Japan; stone or wooden sculptures from Uganda, Zimbabwe and the Solomon Islands, with two ivory carvings (as well as a crocodile handbag and a pair of brass peacocks) from Nigeria, and a fine brass buddha from Nepal. Togo and Grenada both gave stools.

Most of the presents on show in the Throne Room were superbly crafted and expensive, but predictable. Apart from silver tea and coffee sets, silver plates and salvers, canteens of silver and heaps of table glass (four crates of it from the Italian President), there were candlesticks from the King and Queen of Sweden, oriental carpets and rugs from Egypt, India, Bangladesh and Lesotho, several tables and ornamental lamps, a clock from Switzerland, and a silver photograph frame from Their Serene Highnesses the Prince and Princess of Monaco.

Quite a few heads of state solved the present problem by giving paintings or prints, most fairly dull. That from Trinidad and Tobago was a picture of a steel band. The most distinguished, given by the French President, was a painting, *Regattes à Deauville*, by the post-impressionist painter, Raoul Dufy, worth £18,000. Jamaica sent some commemorative stamps with its

gift of a painting, and two gold commemorative coins came from Western Samoa.

The nicest presents must have been the set of garden chairs given by the Queen and Prince of Denmark; the two bedspreads from Tanzania; and the set of grey leather suitcases embossed with C and D from the King and Queen of Spain.

There was little that was personal among the royal and national gifts on display, most of which have found homes in Kensington Palace – the more homely going to Highgrove. But Prince Charles was probably pleased to receive a pair of saddles from the King of Tonga; four sheepskin car-covers from Lesotho; a model yacht from Saint Vincent and the Grenadines, a fifth-century terracotta figurine from Greece; and from Iceland a painting of Vopnafjördur, where every August he used to go salmon-fishing with some friends, including Lord and Lady Tryon.

As all the presents arrived at Buckingham Palace they were laid out in the private cinema. Rear Admiral Sir Hugh Janion, who retired earlier in the year after five years as Flag Officer, Royal Yachts, had been asked by Prince Charles to catalogue, amass and acknowledge the presents. This he did with gusto and with the help of four young ladies and a Georgian library ladder (a wedding present from the bride's aunt,

the Honourable Mrs Michael Gunningham, and her third husband) was put to use at once.

Nearly every day the Prince and his fiancée would visit the cinema to see what had most recently arrived. Singling out the gifts of friends and relatives must have been something of a problem, and very few of these went on display in St James's Palace. Those that did included a picnic basket for six from another aunt of the bride, Lady Anne Wake-Walker, and her husband; a tartan travelling rug from the Princess's 78-year-old great-uncle, Captain the Honourable G.C. Spencer; a video-cassette recorder from Mr and Mrs Tommy Sopwith, skiing friends of the Prince; a botanical print from another of his friends, Lady Camilla Fane; eight blue glass goblets from Sir Maurice and Lady Dorman, whose daughter, Sybil, was an early friend of Prince Charles; four prints of polo scenes from Viscount Cowdray, whose son, Michael Pearson, owns the Cowdray Park estate and polo ground where the Prince is a regular player; a dozen port glasses from the Tarporley Hunt in Cheshire; the Reader's Digest *Encyclopedia of Garden Plants and Flowers* from Sir William and Lady Fellowes, the parents of the bride's brother-in-law, Robert Fellowes; a pair of specially designed silver saltcellars from West Heath School; a Limoges box in the shape of a heart from Caroline Harbord-Hammond, who was at West Heath with Lady Diana; a large Royal Worcester bowl from another friend, Andrew Widdowson, who was paralysed after a rugby accident; a silver vase, sugar-tongs and a bon-bon dish from Miss Helen Lightbody, who was once Prince Charles's nanny; a carriage clock from the Queen Mother's household, and another from the tenants of Sandringham; two prints of Cowes from Lord Maclean, the Lord Chamberlain, and his wife – he supervised all the ceremonial arrangements for the wedding; a large collage of the Hyde Park firework display by the Young England Kindergarten (and an engraved goblet); and two white towelling bath-robes, marked *Charles* and *Diana*, from the youngest bridesmaid, Clementine Hambro.

Details of gifts from most close friends and members of both families have not been disclosed. But it is known that David, Viscount Linley, Princess Margaret's son, presented the couple with a dining-room table which he made himself at Parnham House, the John Makepeace School for Craftsmen in Wood, in Dorset, where he and seventeen other students were on a two-year woodworking course; and that the Queen gave the Princess a diamond tiara that once belonged to Queen

At the State Opening of Parliament on 4 November 1981 the Princess wore the diamond tiara presented to her by the Queen. This tiara has nineteen pearl droplets which hang from lover's knots made of diamonds.

Presents of all descriptions were sent to the royal couple from all over the world.

Mary. The Princess wore it at the State Opening of Parliament in 1981.

Undoubtedly many of the presents received from both families were in the form of jewelry. For her twentieth birthday, the Prince is believed to have given his fiancée gold bracelets, a pearl choker and the gold watch she now wears. It was thought he may have given her the Kermit-like frog that graces the bonnet of her black Ford Escort Ghia. He himself has several mascots. But it was one of her sisters who gave her the mascot – perhaps there is a private joke about a princess who kissed a frog that turned into a prince.

Most of the more expensive presents on show outside the Throne Room in St James's Palace came from a variety of organizations. The Royal Air Force gave a pair of antique decanters housed in a casket of blue leather and embossed in gold. The Royal Navy's gift was a silver punch bowl engraved with Wessex Helicopters and a picture of HMS *Bronington*. All ranks of the Regular and Territorial Army presented a late eighteenth-century mahogany tilt-top breakfast table – and a swimming pool (for Highgrove). Members of

the Royal Warrant Holders Association were lavish with gifts: a television set and video mounted in a reproduction Queen Anne cabinet; a Bang and Olufsen music centre; and a mahogany dining-table with twenty matching chairs. On the other hand, individual Warrant Holders were quite restrained: Wartski, jewelers to the Queen, sent a small silver bell with a Fabergé handle; and Harrods' gift was two red leather travelling cases.

Some presents had to be refused, like the offer of shares in an American oil-well and some land in Bangladesh. So were pets, although Jersey's gift of two cows was accepted. The King of Swaziland's gift of a large stone table, whose weight was such that Palace officials feared it would sink through the floor, could not be displayed. A four-poster bed, from Canada, was too large to go on show. The longest present on display was a windsurfer (from a Nottingham firm), and the smallest a silver thimble. The biggest exhibit was a grand piano from Broadwood, the piano-makers. A nineteenth-century square piano was another musical gift, as was an electric organ. All three will presumably be used to accompany the Prince's cello-playing and the Princess's tap-dancing routines. Another interesting musical gift was a set of door chimes, whose

The new gates at Highgrove were presented to the Prince and Princess of Wales by the people of Tetbury as a wedding present. The local people collected over £2,500 for their gift.

twenty-four ways of saying welcome might find a place above the door of the littlest room in Highgrove.

Presents came from all manner of people and from well-wishers all over the world. Many had been painstakingly handmade – by pensioners, children and disabled people. Other presents were rather eccentric: a record of Matt Munro singing 'Diana'; a disguise set; a striped, hand-knitted camel; a record of Verdi's *Macbeth*; and a glue pen.

More ornaments, books and pictures were on show than anything else. A menagerie of dainty porcelain, glass and china animals could fill every mantelpiece and window-ledge in Highgrove not already occupied by decorated eggs. Rabbits were for some reason the most popular ornamental gifts, with birds and mice as runners up; there was also a crystal frog.

Leading the book list were three bibles (one in Welsh) and a wide selection of worthy books – some bought at cost price and presented by self-congratulatory authors.

Quite a few titles competed in dullness: like *Historic Glenelg, Birthplace of South Australia*; *Mining in Botswana* and *Happiness and How to Find It*. But the apogee of awful worthiness was reached by some of the pictures: the most bathetic of them being a framed *Tribute to the Dog*.

A smaller version of the London exhibition of wedding gifts, including The Dress and the attendants' costumes, began a nine-month regional tour on 10 December 1981 in Cardiff. Some two hundred presents, most of which had not been seen in London, were displayed on the tour which encompassed Edinburgh, Chester, Newcastle, Birmingham, Cambridge, Bournemouth, Truro and Brighton. Proceeds from the tour were donated to charities for sick children at the Princess's request.

Which of the ten thousand wedding presents the couple received will become a familiar part of the household scene at Highgrove and in Kensington Palace? Most of the donors can but imagine. There is, however, no doubt that the people's generosity, unsurpassed in history – the goodwill and caring so obviously displayed in what they gave – honoured each giver as well as the Prince and Princess of Wales.

CHAPTER NINE

Setting a Style

WHEREAS EVERY ROOM in Highgrove and the couple's home in Kensington Palace is now fully stocked with wedding gifts, those of the Princess's personal possessions that occupy more space in cupboards than anything else are *clothes*. She has now acquired more than fifty ballgowns and evening dresses, and three times as many items of daywear – not to mention scores of hats, handbags, shoes and dozens of maternity dresses that she has now thankfully laid aside.

By nature a clean and tidy little girl, she learned in her upbringing about the necessity of a good appearance, whether on formal or informal occasions.

She much admired her mother in this and other matters, and still does. Mother and daughter, apart from being the same height, with long legs and a long stride, and besides marrying men twelve years older than themselves, have much in common – not least a shrewd understanding of character and motive and a strong sense of the absurd. Mrs Shand Kydd, at forty-six, is a positive, outgoing woman, tall and strikingly attractive. She has good taste and judgment in clothes and is never overdressed. At the royal wedding she was one of the best-dressed women there.

Three days after her youngest daughter's engagement was announced, Frances Shand Kydd took Lady Diana to the Bellville Sassoon showroom in Pavilion Road, Knightsbridge. In the weeks that followed the two of them were to be seen striding about other couture houses in Knightsbridge and Bond Street, choosing a new and extensive wardrobe for the fiancée of the Prince of Wales.

Her wardrobe was very expensive, way beyond Lady Diana's own private income of £1,200 a year, and until the wedding her clothes were paid for by her parents. Accordingly, although most were purchased at wholesale prices, the cost of the bride's trousseau was ultimately very high – the average price of a suit or dress being £250 and that of a ballgown £1,000.

Since her marriage, the cost of the Princess's wardrobe has had to be borne by Prince Charles. It has been calculated that even allowing for wholesale

LEFT: *Mrs Shand Kydd, the Princess of Wales' mother, has influenced her youngest daughter's style of dress. She is seen here (left), leaving St Paul's Cathedral after a rehearsal for the wedding, with Mrs Nicholas Gaselee whose daughter, Sarah Jane, was a bridesmaid to Lady Diana.*

RIGHT: *The Princess looked stunning in a Bellville Sassoon taffeta dress on 4 March 1982, at the opening of the Barbican Arts Centre. This houses the new London theatre of the Royal Shakespeare Company, a concert hall for the City's oldest orchestra, the London Symphony Orchestra, a cinema, library and art gallery.*

prices, her clothes and accessories in the first year of her marriage cost him on average about £1,500 a week.

Before the engagement, Lady Diana had been accustomed to shopping around for her clothes, like any other girl of her age and class – in various boutiques and in large stores such as Fenwick, Harvey Nichols and Harrods. The blue silk suit she wore on the afternoon of the engagement day had been bought a week before at Harrods: it was designed by Cojana. With hindsight it seems somewhat staid for a nineteen-year-old girl. But its wearer was anxious to appear in something attractive though suitably formal – for she changed out of the ruby-red velvet suit, red stockings and shoes that she had worn that morning.

Bellville Sassoon's salon in Pavilion Road, Knightsbridge, carries on a family tradition begun by Belinda Bellville's grandmother, Cuckoo Leith, who ran a famous dress-shop in the 1920s. Belinda, married to David Whateley, a city financier, saw David Sassoon's work over twenty years ago at a Royal College of Art dress show and asked him to join her as a designer. Their clients now include many titled and famous ladies such as Princess Alexandra, the Duchess of Kent and the Countess of Lichfield.

Before her engagement she frequently wore separates, chosen with a good eye for contrasting and complementary colours and textures. She liked long skirts, hand-knitted jerseys and cardigans, Edwardian-style blouses with high necks and frills, cravats and culottes. In her Coleherne Court wardrobe were cardigans from Friends, lambswool pullovers from Benetton, Fiorucci sweatshirts, cotton shirts and skirts from Laura Ashley, and suits and evening dresses from Harvey Nichols and Harrods. Some items were borrowed from friends, including her sisters. Her most unorthodox possessions were a man's corduroy smoking-jacket, a trilby and a man's watch.

Always slightly self-conscious about her height – 5 ft 10¼ ins – she wore low-heeled shoes, and she never wore hats. Also fashion-conscious, she read and studied *Harpers* and *Vogue*, as well as *Woman*, picking up ideas and adopting those that suited her style – like blouses with frilly necks and sleeves, knickerbockers, Provençal print dresses, eye-veils on hats, and what was known in 1981 as the 'romantic look'.

After the engagement was announced, Mrs Shand Kydd introduced Lady Diana to fashion designers Bill Pashley, Jean Muir, and milliner John Boyd – as well as to Bellville Sassoon.

The partnership of Belinda Bellville and David Sassoon has to date provided most of the outfits, dresses, coats and gowns designed for the Princess since her engagement and wedding. About twenty-five of Bellville Sassoon's creations have been worn by her in public, most notably the sailor suit she wore in March 1981 for her first official photographs with the Queen and Prince Charles; the red and silver chiffon ball dress seen at the Gala Première in London of *For Your Eyes Only* on 24 June; the coral pink dress and jacket worn as a going-away outfit on 29 July; the hand-painted chiffon crinoline displayed at the 'Splendours of the Gonzaga' Exhibition on 4 November; and the red tweed coat and blue three-piece outfit worn at the Guildhall on 5 November, the day it was announced she was expecting a child.

Another fifteen or so dresses made by Bellville Sassoon for the Princess have not been publicly seen, but she has worn several of the maternity dresses they designed for her, as well as the velour coats and gorgeous evening dresses seen in February and March 1982 – at Westminster Abbey, at a Hampshire wedding; and at the Barbican Centre, the Victoria Palace Theatre and the Royal Albert Hall.

Bill Pashley's haute couture clothes are unique in that he designs, cuts and sews them all himself. 'I don't employ anyone else,' he says. 'Each garment is entirely designed and made by me. I just enjoy designing and making clothes, and after twenty-five years it still feels like a hobby.' His country clothes are particularly admired by his titled clientele, and he made more than a dozen items for the Princess of Wales when she was Lady Diana. He designed the houndstooth check tweed suit worn by her at the photo-session at Balmoral in August 1981; the tobacco-brown flannel suit she wore at Sandown Park Racecourse on 13 March; the cherry-red wool coat seen later that month at Heathrow Airport; and the printed cotton shirt and quilted waistcoat worn at Tidworth in June. He also makes capes, coats and evening dresses – his Loden capes have been much worn by the Princess out of town.

Several outfits designed by top couturier, Jean Muir, were bought by the Princess after her marriage and

BELOW: Bill Pashley, a 47-year-old Yorkshireman, was a contemporary of David Sassoon at the Royal College of Art. He works from his home in Battersea – a house crammed with objets d'art, including a fine collection of early Victorian hand-painted papier-mâché boxes and trays inlaid with mother-of-pearl. Pashley's constant companion is a 14-year-old beagle called Sybil.
RIGHT: Lady Diana favoured pretty prints as a teenager. She is seen here at a polo match at Tidworth wearing a Bill Pashley printed cotton skirt with matching waistcoat. Her lilac kid shoes were designed by Alexander Gabbay of Ivory.

she has been pictured in two of them: a green wool crêpe cape, worn at Heathrow Airport on 3 September 1981; and an emerald-green suede jacket and skirt (the jacket trimmed in gold punched leather) which were worn at a concert in Tetbury's parish church on 6 December 1981.

The Princess distinguishes between what is suitable for her to wear in public and what she wears in private. In neither case does she follow royal convention, except in the wearing of hats. For these she goes to John Boyd's little millinery shop in Brompton Arcade. He is a soft-spoken, humorous native of Edinburgh, which he left to join the Navy, and he learned his trade from Aage Thaarup, the Queen Mother's milliner. He treats his young but beautiful and distinguished customer – and he has several such others – as if she were a Scottish lass. For the past year he has been experimenting at her suggestion with various styles and trimmings, and she has been learning how to wear the hats he makes for her. He says, 'She doesn't always put her hats on properly . . . She'll come in and say,

John Boyd, the Princess's milliner, and some of his magnificent hats. He works from a small shop in Knightsbridge.

"You must be so cross with me – how I put it on yesterday." But I always tell her that she's learning fast.' His sister helps him in his business.

In the matter of matching his hats to the colour of her suits, the Princess has seldom let him see the whole outfit, and he usually creates the hats, doing his own dyeing, with just a scrap of fabric or a belt for guidance. Quite a few have been duplicated in different colours, such as the feather-trimmed hat worn on the Welsh tour in October 1981. Others have been retrimmed, like the red straw hat originally worn at the Soames' wedding, and then, with a difference and a green ribbon, in Wales. All have to be tightly pinned to her hair so they will not budge in a strong wind. The most eye-catching of his hats, which cost up to £65, have been those of a tricorn style and worn with a jaunty tilt.

'She'll always be just a wee lassie to me,' says Mr Boyd, 'a young girl thrilled with a wee bit of veil or feather.' Prince Charles also likes to see his wife in eye-veils, and John Boyd sometimes dyes the edge of the veils blue to match her eyes.

In choosing hats as well as clothes the Princess tends to make swift if not instant decisions. One designer was sent a hat belonging to her sister, Lady Sarah, and

ABOVE: *The Princess sometimes has her hats retrimmed. John Boyd's red straw hat was retrimmed for the tour of Wales in October 1981. The Princess wore it previously at Nicholas Soames' wedding in June 1981.*

BELOW: *Donald Campbell, a quiet middle-aged Canadian, trained with designer John Cavanagh. Among his many distinguished clients are Princess Alexandra and the Duchess of Kent.*

asked to produce an outfit that would go with it the following day. When shopping for clothes the Princess will see a dress she likes and then have it made up in another colour, even in another fabric. On occasions she changes a sash or a collar, or has outfits altered to suit her liking for long, slim-line skirts and small waists. She is not afraid of new fashions, or of adapting the 'in-look' to suit herself. Choosing clothes still has an element of fun for her. Indeed, she does not think that clothes should be taken too seriously and keeps fittings to a minimum.

Tall and slim, with attributes that many a model would envy – a svelte size 10–12, long legs, a 22-inch waist, fine features and an ideal complexion – the Princess shows the clothes she wears to their best advantage. She would look good, say her designers, in anything, and it is with pride and delight that they see her pictured in their designs.

It was not the Princess's mother, but her sister, Lady Jane, who took her to Donald Campbell's smart salon in William Street, Knightsbridge, three months after the engagement. To date, the Princess has purchased about twenty of his off-the-peg dresses, made with the delicate hand-stitched features of haute couture. The Princess of Wales attracted much admiring appreciation when she wore his dresses on five of her public engagements in the latter half of 1981. They included the floral printed *façonnée* crêpe-de-Chine

ABOVE: *The Princess of Wales wore Donald Campbell's romantic floral printed* façonnée crêpe-de-Chine *dress and jacket at the start of the honeymoon cruise in Gibraltar.*
BELOW RIGHT: *Caroline Charles was apprenticed to the English couturier Michael Sherard, and to Mary Quant. She is known for her exquisite fabrics and her clients include Princess Margaret, the Duchess of Kent and the Queen of Jordan. She runs her business from Beauchamp Place in Knightsbridge.*

dress and jacket that she wore at Gibraltar before embarking on the honeymoon cruise; the red and green jacket and skirt worn on the first day of the Welsh tour, at Rhyl and Caernarvon; the blue and gold striped chiffon dress seen at the City Hall in Cardiff; and the poppy-printed green and black dress worn at Chesterfield on 12 November 1981.

Of her current couturiers, she has been wearing clothes designed by Caroline Charles longer than anyone else, some having been bought off the peg months before she became engaged. Few, however, have yet been seen in public, the most photographed having been the red and black plaid wool and cotton suit (costing £240) which the Princess wore to the Braemar Games in September 1981, and the sand-coloured cashmere coat and matching skirt with a ruffled silk blouse

RIGHT: *On 16 June 1981 at Royal Ascot Lady Diana wore a pretty multi-coloured three-piece creation designed by Neil and Fortescue. The outfit was made of crêpe de Chine and consisted of a jacket with a pleated collar, a camisole top and a matching pleated skirt.*

that were worn on the second day of the Welsh tour, at St David's and Haverfordwest.

Also popular with the Princess is the designing team of David Neil and Julia Fortescue. The most photographed creation of theirs worn by the Princess, who was introduced to their designs by *Vogue*, was the red silk two-piece outfit in which she appeared at the wedding of the Honourable Nicholas Soames and Catherine Weatherall on 4 June 1981. One of her outfits for Ascot that month was also designed by Neil and Fortescue: a multi-coloured three-piece in silk crêpe de Chine.

Vogue was also responsible for drawing the Princess's eye to the creations of Gina Fratini. At a photo-session organized by *Vogue* at the beginning of 1981, Lady Diana was pictured by Snowdon wearing a cream organza ballgown designed by Gina Fratini. It was borrowed for the session, but later presented to the Princess. Since then she has appeared in a Gina Fratini black velvet cape on the Welsh tour; a dark green velvet dress with a puritan white lace collar at the opening of the London Film Festival on 3 November; and a burgundy striped taffeta long dress which had a velvet strapless bodice and was worn under a matching jacket.

For the Snowdon photo-session, as with others and also on her wedding day, the Princess was made-up by

David Neil and Julia Fortescue work from a small set of rooms in South Molton Street in London's West End. They worked previously with Collection O in Walton Street. They show their collections twice a year and specialize in wedding dresses. Their clients include the Duchess of Westminster and Lady Romsey – wife of Prince Charles's cousin.

Barbara Daly. The resulting photographs were apparently not much to the Princess's liking – she thought she looked too artificial and 'waxy'. Preferring a more natural look, she normally wears very little make-up. The cosmetics she uses include Clinique lipstick, and Boots No. 7 Marshmallow and Lilyroot Moisturising Cream. She has her eyelashes tinted, and her hair, which she carefully tends, is finely highlighted – with 'Di-lights' as American newspapers call them. More recently she has worn it longer.

Her hairdresser is Kevin Shanley, aged twenty-seven. A West Londoner, of Irish origins, he was trained at Dorothy Gray in Conduit Street and began cutting the Princess's hair when she was a schoolgirl and he was working at Fenwick in Bond Street. She was following in the steps of her sisters, Lady Sarah and Lady Jane, and when he moved to Head Lines Hair

and Beauty Salon in South Kensington (in which he is now a partner) they followed him. Mrs Shand Kydd is another of his customers; and since the wedding he has regularly cut Prince Charles's hair in Buckingham Palace.

Head Lines is not a 'debby' place, being rather plain and functional, where a haircut can cost £15 and highlights £27, and Kevin is a straight-forward, non-camp man. 'I go to Buckingham Palace and Balmoral,' he says, 'places like that. It did seem a bit different at first, but it's just work now. I'm not in awe or anything like that . . . No one ever told me what to say or what not to say, and I've appreciated that . . . Anyway, I'm not the type to put on an act. If I was, I wouldn't be where I am today, and that should tell you something.'

The Princess still drops in at Head Lines to have her hair done and to recapture some of the easy unstructured life she knew before her engagement. When her public duties are many, Kevin is called in to see her as often as four times a week. She has remained with him, despite the fact that she could have her hair dressed by any hair stylist in Britain. 'She liked my work,' says Kevin, 'so I wasn't surprised when she stayed with me. I'd have been more surprised if she'd changed.' He still calls her Diana.

The Princess has followed in the steps of her two older sisters in other respects. Both used to work for *Vogue* before their marriages, and the magazine's beauty editor, Felicity Clark, is a particular friend of theirs. Acting as intermediaries, *Vogue*'s fashion editors have since the engagement introduced the Princess to clothes designed by Emanuel, Jasper Conran, Roland Klein, Bruce Oldfield, Gina Fratini, David Neil and Julia Fortescue, Benny Ong, and to those made by wholesale companies like Nettie Vogues, Jaeger, the Chelsea Design Company and Salvador. 'The idea has been,' says Felicity Clark, 'to bring the best of British fashion under her eye and to help her . . . But we only present clothes as though she were in a shop and then she chooses what she likes.'

Vogue provides a similar service for the Duchess of Kent and Princess Michael, who visit the Hanover Square offices to preview the latest fashions.

The Emanuel connection arose out of the Snowdon photo-session for *Vogue*, when Lady Diana was photographed wearing, besides the Gina Fratini ballgown, a palest pink silk chiffon blouse that had been designed by David and Elizabeth Emanuel. A visit to their wall-mirrored Brook Street showroom followed, as did commissions for several ballgowns, and ultimately the wedding dress. Only two of the gowns have been seen in public: the strapless low-cut black silk taffeta ballgown displayed at the Goldsmiths' Hall; and a pale blue sequinned tulle dress with fitted sleeves that the Princess wore at Claridge's for the dinner given by King Khaled. She has also worn Emanuel ballgowns at Prince Andrew's twenty-first birthday dance in Windsor Castle and at the Palace ball held two days before the wedding. But since the wedding it seems that the large degree of self-promotion undertaken by the Emanuels has been offputting to the Princess. With

---

Kevin Shanley, hairdresser to the Princess of Wales, is married with a one-year-old daughter called Melissa. He has been dressing the Princess's blonde hair for the last five years, giving it a virtually unchanged high-layered club cut.

The Emanuels' beautiful drawing of the wedding dress for Lady Diana Spencer. The frilled neckline, the full and gathered sleeves, the lace flounces and taffeta bows, and the embroidered lace panels completed the romantic fantasy.

the help of a top publicity agent, Mark McCormack, Emanuel began marketing scent, sunglasses and expensive bed-linen – and the Princess is believed not to have visited their salon again.

It is also now evident, despite the instant rapture that greeted the first public view of the wedding dress, that it was ultimately something of a disappointment. This, of course, was almost bound to happen as expectations ran so high. But the crushed effect of the taffeta skirt, the bulky effect of the sleeves, the less than virginal white of the whole ensemble, seem in reflection like flaws. Perhaps the Princess herself was aware, as she watched the video-tape recordings of the marriage service, of the discrepancy between the designers' beautiful drawings of the dress and the reality.

Since the wedding the younger, less established designers whose clothes she has worn have become wary of publicity and of saying too much, in case the Princess's patronage may be withdrawn. *Vogue's* editors have also become very remote.

Jasper Conran's precocious confidence, however, has not been dimmed. He has moved into light and airy new premises in Great Marlborough Street. He was one of the chief providers, along with Bellville Sassoon, Caroline Charles, Gina Fratini, David Neil and Julia Fortescue, of maternity dresses for the Princess of Wales – tailored dresses, with collars and frills, and latterly the more usual maternity-wear of waistless smocks. Before that, although he had provided the Princess with several party dresses, his photographed clothes included a white silk and wool skirt with a white mohair jacket, and the red-and-white spotted silk jacket and red silk skirt seen at Tetbury on 22 May 1981.

Another designer drawn to the Princess's attention by *Vogue* was the 32-year-old half-Jamaican, Bruce Oldfield. One of his outfits was worn by the Princess when she switched on the Christmas lights in Regent Street on 18 November. Suits and dresses have also been purchased from the ready-to-wear fashion house of Marcel Fenez, run by French designer, Roland Klein.

Under *Vogue's* aegis, the Princess also chose Jaeger's burgundy velvet suit with a black-embroidered waisted jacket that was seen on the last day of the Welsh tour; and the emerald-green taffeta ballgown made by Nettie Vogues that she wore for the official engagement pictures taken by Snowdon. The gown, designed by Graham Wren for Nettie Vogues, has elasticated sleeves that can be worn on or off the shoulder. In fact, most of the Princess's dresses were elasticated so that they could be worn well into her pregnancy.

Notwithstanding the suggestions and advice of her mother, her sisters and *Vogue*, the Princess has remained Mistress of her own Robes. She continues to visit Harrods, Harvey Nichols, dress-shops, and boutiques such as Chanel. In the early summer of 1981 she bought a white Crombie-style coat in pure wool flannel off-the-peg (for £149) from Courtenay in Brook Street and wore it at the end of her honeymoon. Some of her colourful jerseys and jumpers have come from shops like Benetton and Inca, and James Drew blouses from boutiques like Brother Sun. Just before Christmas 1981 she visited the Prince's shirtmakers, Turnbull and Asser, to choose some shirts for him. She also ordered several for herself (plain, striped and checked), to be worn with casual trousers and jeans.

Her shoes used to be purchased directly from shops such as Jourdan, The Chelsea Cobbler and Zapata in Kensington. But since the wedding – for which Clive Shilton designed her wedding shoes – she has had shoes made for her by the Queen's shoemaker, Edward Rayne; by Manolo Blahnik; and by Alexander Gabbay of Ivory, who made the bridesmaids' shoes. Most of her honeymoon shoes were bought at Harrods. She has invariably worn a court shoe with a two-inch heel or less – not necessarily because of her height, but because flat shoes have been fashionable. The shoes she wears (size 6–6½) are unfussy, in one colour kid, usually ornamented with some slight feature or subtle piping. But the matching bags that are provided with the shoes are not always worn as such.

The Princess will continue to mould current fashions to suit her own style. For the time being she will follow

LEFT: *Jasper Conran, aged twenty-two, is the son of Terence and 'Superwoman' Shirley Conran. He designed several maternity dresses for the Princess and sketches for one can be seen on the left in the photograph.*
RIGHT: *This study of the Prince of Wales and his fiancée was taken by Snowdon at Highgrove. Lady Diana wore an emerald green taffeta ballgown with elasticated sleeves; she also wore this gown, designed by Nettie Vogues, to a Gala Concert in Swansea in October 1981. The diamond necklace and earrings, borrowed for the photograph, were sold in Dusseldorf, West Germany, in March 1982 at the inflated price of £65,000.*

ABOVE: *The Princess of Wales loves colourful jumpers –
like the sheep one she is wearing here. It was bought by a
friend from Warm and Wonderful.*
LEFT: *The Princess in setting a style is beginning to
concentrate on a few of her favourite designers – such
as Bellville Sassoon, who designed the velour coat she
wore to Liverpool on 2 April 1982.*
BELOW: *The Princess of Wales' wedding slippers were
created by Clive Shilton. They were made of ivory silk,
top-stitched and covered with mother-of-pearl sequins.
The front of the shoes bore a lace rosette with
ruffled edges around a heart-shaped design piped in
gold leather, which in turn was covered with pearls
and sequins. The soles were made of suede and edged
with gold. The under-arches were hand-painted with
gold motifs.*

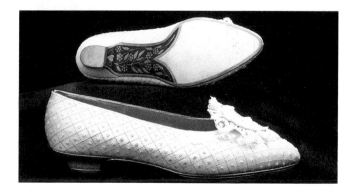

fashion rather than lead it, none the less setting a style
for others to follow by appropriating aspects of fashion
which she likes. Her accessories have had more
imitators than her dresses – her hats, her pearl chokers,
her capes and muffs.

Since her engagement she has sometimes been
criticized for being 'frumpy' or for being unduly
influenced by Palace opinion. This is not so. While
wishing to look her best when appearing in public, she
has also no wish to excite undue interest or comment.
Like any other girl, she dresses for the occasion. All
her occasions happen to be *royal*, and she dresses
accordingly – in what is also fashionable, colourful and
attractive.

Sometimes she makes mistakes. She will not be seen
again in public, for instance, in such a low-cut strapless
dress as the black ballgown she wore at the Goldsmiths'
Hall. It aroused the wrong sort of press and photographic attention. Unaccustomed as she was to the
wearing of hats, necessary adornments on formal
occasions, she has sometimes also chosen wrongly or
worn them in the wrong way. The large tam o' shanter
she donned for the Braemar Games was not very
becoming, and a similar creation worn in Northampton
in November made her look, according to one designer,
'like somebody's aunt'. The red straw hat worn at the
Soames' wedding was stylishly tilted and right; the
same hat adapted for the Welsh visit and worn further
back on her head was not so successful.

Self-critical, she studies her image as portrayed in
newspapers and magazines and objectively makes
adjustments, asking for the opinion of others (even of
her police bodyguards) to confirm her own of herself.
It should be remembered that although she is blessed
with natural beauty and an excellent figure, she is still
quite young and her experience not large. But as her
mother said at the time of the engagement, 'I'm sure
she can cope and will learn very quickly.'

In matters of fashion, the first royal year of the
Princess of Wales has been, among other things, a time
of learning and judicious experiment – as well as a
tremendous boost to Britain's rag trade. Soon her taste
in clothes and accessories will become more defined and
even impeccable. She will concentrate on a few tried
and tested designers, with occasional excursions to
others, and on the establishing of a style and styles of
her own.

CHAPTER TEN

Her Royal Highness

THE STYLE AND TITLE of the Princess of Wales is that, just that – not Princess Diana or even Diana, Princess of Wales. These forms of address are incorrect. And she was never called Di by her family or friends. That name was invented by the vulgar press.

She is royal by marriage, not by birth. Therefore, as wife of the Prince of Wales, she becomes his Princess – as well as his Countess of Chester, Duchess of Cornwall, Duchess of Rothesay, Countess of Carrick, Baroness of Renfrew and, as wife of the eldest son of the sovereign, Her Royal Highness. As Princess of Wales, her name has now been added to the Liturgy of the Church of England. She could become Queen, but she will never rule the country.

Her family surname, Spencer, has been superceded, as has her former title, Lady Diana. She now signs her name, both privately and officially, as *Diana*. Her husband privately signs himself *Charles*. But on official documents he writes *Charles P* – the P standing

---

The official entry of the solemnization of the royal couple's marriage in St Paul's marriage register. The Prince of Wales signs himself as Charles P *on official documents and the Princess herself simply as* Diana. *The Queen and Elizabeth the Queen Mother both sign themselves* Elizabeth R.

for 'Princeps' or 'Prince'. His mother and grandmother both sign themselves *Elizabeth R* ('Regina', or 'Queen').

Until he was three and a half, Prince Charles did not have an official surname. But in April 1952 his mother declared, 'I and my children shall be styled and known as the House and Family of Windsor' – as would her descendants. Thereupon her eldest (and then only) son became in the eyes of the law Charles Windsor. But as his father, a naturalized British subject, was only a Duke – having been created Duke of Edinburgh, Earl of Merioneth and Baron of Greenwich in 1947, on the day he married the then Princess Elizabeth – special Letters Patent were drawn up to make his son a Prince, and his daughter a Princess. Royal children take their titles from their father, not their mother.

In February 1960 the Queen elaborated her decree of 1952 and, wishing to commemorate her husband's name in some way, declared that those of her descendants who were not princes or princesses should bear the surname Mountbatten-Windsor.

Prince Charles need not call himself King Charles III when he becomes King. One of his first acts on acceding to the throne will be to choose the name by which he will be known in history. He could choose any of his other names – Philip I, Arthur II or George VII – or something different like John II or William V.

At the moment, in the list of social precedence, the Princess of Wales is the third lady in the land, after the Queen and the Queen Mother and preceding Princess Margaret and Princess Anne. Except on the most formal occasions, she is not required to curtsey to either the Queen or the Queen Mother, her more usual and affectionate greeting or farewell, a kiss on the cheek, being used instead, even in public – something that was last done by another Princess of Wales, Princess Alexandra. Nor will any other member of the royal family be expected to curtsey to her. Mrs Shand Kydd, a baron's daughter, has never been required to curtsey before her own daughter, the Princess of Wales. Earl Spencer chose to bow his head before her when as Princess she visited Althorp in November 1981. But within the royal family formalities are few.

With the arrival of the Princess of Wales, the democratization of royalty will probably proceed apace. Perhaps before long even commoners will be less distanced from royalty by court rituals and protocol and ultimately only by their aristocratic life-style and enormous wealth.

Her Royal Highness the Princess of Wales attended her first State ceremony, with the Prince of Wales, on 4 November 1981, when the Queen opened the new session of Parliament in the Lords Chamber. Prince Philip, Princess Anne and Captain Mark Phillips were also present.

CHAPTER ELEVEN

Court Circular

THE COURT CIRCULAR, which has listed the royal family's official engagements and movements since 1785, is issued by the Lord Steward at Buckingham Palace and published in *The Times* and *Daily Telegraph*. The Princess of Wales made her first appearance in its columns on *17 August 1981*, when it was reported that two days earlier, 'The Prince and Princess of Wales arrived at Balmoral Castle this evening.' As Lady Diana Spencer, she was first named in the Court Circular on *9 March 1981*, when she and Prince Charles attended a recital at the Goldsmiths' Hall, London.

After the tour of Wales ended, entries concerning the Princess in the Court Circular stated that on the evening of Sunday, *1 November*, she and the Prince attended an English Heritage Concert at Blenheim Palace, home of the Duke of Marlborough: that at 8 p.m. on *3 November* they went to the National Film Theatre, to open the 25th London Film Festival and see the film *Gallipoli*; that on the morning of Wednesday, *4 November*, the Prince and Princess of Wales were both present at the State Opening of Parliament; and that at 6.30 that evening they opened the 'Splendours of the Gonzaga' Exhibition of Italian Renaissance art held in the Victoria and Albert Museum, South Kensington, in London.

Both occasions that day were splendidly regal, sumptuous affairs, and the Princess's appearance was entirely in keeping with them. It was the first time since her wedding that she had attended a State occasion or been driven in the Glass Coach. She looked stunning. But at both occasions she seemed abashed, even overawed, clutching her handbag during the Queen's Speech, scarcely daring to look up or around, and at the Exhibition gazing wistfully about. If she appeared to be unduly self-conscious, it was probably because of the impending announcement of her pregnancy. As it was, after the Exhibition she withdrew from a dinner engagement at the Italian Embassy, affording the Ambassador's wife, Signora Cagiati, who alone knew the reason for this, the chance to be at her most diplomatic in parrying questions about the Princess's absence.

The following morning, at eleven o'clock on Thursday, *5 November*, the Palace announced that the Princess of Wales was expecting a baby in June. The statement said:

> The Prince and Princess of Wales, the Queen and the Duke of Edinburgh and members of both families are delighted by the news. The Queen was informed personally by the Prince and Princess. The Princess is in excellent health. Her doctor during the pregnancy will be Mr George Pinker, Surgeon-Gynaecologist to the Queen. The Princess hopes to continue to undertake some public engagements, but regrets any disappointment which may be caused by any curtailment of her planned programme. The baby will be second in line to the Throne.

Mrs Shand Kydd was said to be 'absolutely overjoyed' and Earl Spencer 'absolutely thrilled'.

The early announcement of the Princess's pregnancy was mainly due to the fact that visits by the Prince and his wife to Australia, New Zealand and Canada, provisionally planned for 1982, could be openly postponed before any further arrangements were made.

Two hours after the announcement, the Prince and Princess were guests of honour at a luncheon given by the Lord Mayor and Corporation of the City of London at the Guildhall to thank the couple for choosing St Paul's for their wedding service. The Lord Mayor, Sir Ronald Gardner-Thorpe, told the couple, 'The wedding provided a memory that glows like an ingot. That ingot has now been hallmarked by the news that you are to be blessed with a child.' There was loud applause – as well as delighted cries from the six hundred guests of 'Bravo, Sir!' 'Jolly good show!' and 'Congratulations!' The Princess blushed. The Lord Mayor continued, 'We all rejoice, remembering that babies are

On 3 November the Princess attended the opening of the 25th London Film Festival. She wore a dark green velvet dress with a puritan lace collar and an attached lace petticoat designed by Gina Fratini.

11.00 hrs
PA FLASH
 Princess of Wales expecting baby in June, Buckingham
Palace announced.
End Flash 1100 rf
NNN A Princess of Wales

"By the right ... quick knit!"

Isn't it too soon to start knitting them little booties?

The Right Honourable the Lord Mayor and the Corporation of the City of London entertained the Prince and Princess of Wales at luncheon at the Guildhall on 5 November 1981 – the day it was announced the Princess was expecting a baby the following summer.

bits of stardust blown from the land of God.' Earlier, the Prince had said, as he arrived at the Guildhall with his wife, 'Naturally I'm absolutely delighted . . . And of course I feel like any prospective father. My wife is overjoyed as well. A baby will be marvellous.' His wife was suddenly camera-shy.

The song 'Congratulations' was sung for the Prince and Princess by the large audience attending and participating in the 60th Anniversary of the Royal British Legion's Festival of Remembrance at the Royal Albert Hall on the evening of Saturday, *7 November.* That morning in Gloucestershire, the Princess had worn quite a different garb, an anorak and jeans, when she drove into Tetbury from Highgrove to visit a newsagent and buy a magazine, the local paper and some sweets.

On Sunday, the royal family attended the ceremony at the Cenotaph in Whitehall commemorating the dead of two world wars. After the two-minute silence that followed the chimes of Big Ben at eleven o'clock, the Queen, Prince Philip, Prince Charles, the Duke of Kent and Prince Michael all laid wreaths. Security was very strict: people in the crowds nearest the Cenotaph were searched. The Princess of Wales watched the ceremony from a balcony in the old Home Office.

The Princess attended the Remembrance Sunday ceremony at the Cenotaph on 8 November with King Olav of Norway (left), Princess Alice, and the Queen Mother (right). Her black suit and white satin blouse were designed by Bellville Sassoon.

Standing with the Queen Mother, King Olav of Norway and Princess Alice, she seemed somewhat tense – as if in anticipation of the morning sickness that would afflict her. Her attendance at the Remembrance Day Service at the Guards Chapel that afternoon had already been cancelled. A friend said, 'Poor Diana. She doesn't just suffer from morning sickness – it's an all-day job with her.'

The following night a visit to the Duchy of Cornwall's estates in Devon, scheduled for Tuesday – the Princess's first as Duchess of Cornwall – was also cancelled. 'You all have wives – you know what it's like,' said the Prince to disappointed tenants. But by Thursday, *12 November*, she seemed fit enough to undertake a visit with her husband in the Royal Train to York, where she made a ninety-minute tour of the National Railway Museum, doggedly climbing in and out of railway carriages, before driving around York's Rugby League ground to be cheered by seven thousand children. The couple then flew by helicopter on to

Chesterfield in Derbyshire, where large crowds greeted them at the Town Hall after the Prince opened a new £12-million shopping centre. At the end of the day, after three walkabouts and much handshaking, the Princess looked exhausted. She told a woman in the crowd, 'Some days I feel terrible. Nobody told me I'd feel like this.'

The Prince was much concerned, and it was decided that his young wife would do no more walkabouts and fulfil only one engagement a day. However, throughout the months of her pregnancy, the bouts of sickness continued to trouble her.

That weekend they were at Wood Farm, Sandringham, for Prince Charles's birthday on Saturday, *14 November*: he was thirty-three. He went out pheasant-shooting and the Princess accompanied him, wearing stereo headphones attached to a Sony Walkman portable cassette-player and listening to some

On 12 November the royal couple visited Chesterfield, where Prince Charles opened a new shopping development which includes the largest open-air market in England. The Princess was clearly feeling unwell but insisted on accompanying her husband. She wore a dress of fine wool challis printed with poppies, designed by Donald Campbell, under a black cape.

music. They celebrated his birthday with a dinner-party that evening at Wood Farm, and on Sunday stayed at home, disappointing the crowds who had gathered to see them at Sandringham Church.

On Monday morning they were the guests of Hugh and Emilie van Cutsem at a pheasant-drive on the van Cutsems' estate near Newmarket in Suffolk, after which the Prince and Princess drove across country to Highgrove. That night, however, the Princess cancelled a visit to Bristol scheduled for Tuesday. The Palace said that although she was 'otherwise in excellent health', she was suffering from morning sickness, and having accepted medical advice had regretfully decided she could not accompany the Prince. He visited a factory, a primary school and a community centre on his own and attended a charity concert.

The Princess returned to London on Wednesday, *18 November*, to switch on the Christmas illuminations in Regent Street. Arriving outside the Austin Reed store, where thousands of people had gathered in the rain, she appeared – for the first time without her husband – on a balcony above the street. Before the 'switch-on' she made a brief and rapidly spoken speech. She said, 'It is very kind of the Regent Street Association to invite me to switch on the Christmas lights this year, and I am delighted to have this opportunity of making a small contribution to the Christmas spirit in London. I know these lights give a great deal of pleasure to countless people in the weeks leading up to 25 December – particularly to families who bring their children to see them . . .'

At a reception afterwards, while sipping soda water, she told well-wishers, 'I'm fine – I'm feeling much better,' and she said to singer, Cilla Black, 'I see you've brought your other half with you. I've left mine at home watching the TV.'

The following morning at Buckingham Palace, while the Prince of Wales received the Lord Warden of the Stannaries and the retiring Colonel of the 1st Battalion, the Parachute Regiment, the Princess had her first experience of similar tasks, which will come to be among her most regular royal duties. She received the Master and Clerk of the Worshipful Company of

Fanmakers. Later, she and the Prince planted three trees in Hyde Park commemorating their marriage – the third was for their expected baby – before being entertained to lunch at the Royal Thames Yacht Club in Knightsbridge.

On Friday, *20 November*, the Princess flew by helicopter to Althorp, landing on the gravel in front of her father's ancestral home. She had lunch with him and Countess Spencer before being driven in his Rolls-Royce into Northampton where she opened the city's new £7-million Head Post Office. She was rapturously received by a crowd of nearly ten thousand people, including hundreds of children. At the Post Office, she sent a congratulatory telegram to the Queen and Prince Philip on the thirty-fourth anniversary of their marriage, posted a letter to Highgrove, and met the postman, Frank Barringer, who had delivered mail for eighteen years to Althorp. She also made a speech, her third as Princess of Wales.

After another weekend spent at Highgrove, the Princess was spotted once more in Tetbury, casually dressed and again buying sweets. Elsewhere, Prince Charles was out hunting with the Beaufort. The day before, it had been announced that he had sold his steeplechaser, Good Prospect, because a variety of commitments prevented him from competing again that season. His jaunts as a jockey were over.

LEFT: *A small boy presented a bouquet to the Princess on 19 November when she and Prince Charles planted three trees in Hyde Park to commemorate their marriage and the birth of their first child the following year.*
RIGHT: *The people of Tetbury were delighted when the Prince and Princess of Wales, with their weekend guests, attended a concert in aid of the Benjamin Britten fund for young musicians in the parish church on 6 December 1981. The Princess wore a green suede jacket and skirt designed by Jean Muir. The jacket was trimmed with punched gold leather.*

By *24 November* the couple were back in London, staying at Buckingham Palace. That night the Princess was indisposed and unable to attend a Reception at the Palace given by the Queen and Prince Philip for Members of the Diplomatic Corps. The following evening, however, she and the Prince, accompanied by Prince Andrew and Viscount Linley, by her two sisters and their husbands, went to the Royal Opera House, Covent Garden, to see the ballet, *Romeo and Juliet*, after which they went backstage to meet the company. Five days later the Prince and Princess made a private return visit to the Royal Opera House to see the last night of *Tosca*.

On *1 December*, on a cold but sunny Tuesday morning, the Princess was with her husband and her parents-in-law at Buckingham Palace when they presented cars to disabled people in the Motability Scheme. That night the couple went, with Edward Adeane and Anne Beckwith-Smith, to the House of Commons to dine with the Speaker, George Thomas, and senior politicians. During the dinner, the Labour M.P. for West Lothian, incensed that the business of the day had been curtailed two hours ahead of time – thus wrecking his hoped-for debate on factory closures – demanded that another debate be initiated. Division bells were rung, recalling M.P.s to the House to settle the issue, and the royal couple were left alone with the Speaker, as his guests, including the Prime Minister, hurriedly left the banquet.

That same day the Palace announced that the Princess of Wales would not accompany the Prince on his visit the next day to Cornwall – nor to the Chippenham Fatstock Show dinner the following Monday. So on *2 December* the Prince again visited Duchy property without his Duchess. At Falmouth, where he opened a new coastguard rescue centre, a plaque had to be hastily replaced by one bearing his name alone. He told the audience there, 'I've come to the conclusion most ladies think we men don't understand the problems they face. But I must say I am slowly beginning to find out what these are.'

But four days later, on Sunday, *6 December*, the Princess was able to attend a concert in aid of the Britten Foundation at Tetbury's parish church. She arrived at the floodlit church with the Prince and their weekend house-guests, Lord Patrick Beresford and Mr and Mrs Nicholas Soames. Other guests that weekend had been Lady Sarah McCorquodale and her husband, Neil.

The royal couple were at Highgrove for more than a fortnight in December, the longest they had ever spent there together. They entertained friends and fulfilled a few engagements, settling into their new home and enjoying some leisure on their snow-covered estate – there were unusually heavy snowfalls in Britain that month. On Tuesday, *8 December*, the Princess drove herself through falling snow from Highgrove to St Mary's Church of England Primary School in Tetbury, fulfilling a promise to make an informal visit after her marriage. After hearing the entire school of 330 children sing two carols at morning assembly, she visited classrooms bright with Christmas decorations and chatted to the staff.

Later that morning, in London, an unprecedented convocation of the editors of national newspapers and radio and television news programmes, was invited to assemble at Buckingham Palace by the Queen's Press Secretary, Michael Shea. The only editor who failed to attend was that of *The Sun*. The Queen was concerned about the photographic and press intrusion on the Princess's private life, especially at Highgrove, and although long accustomed herself to obsessive press attention, was averse to the wishes and movements of her daughter-in-law being unduly inhibited and restricted. If the Princess wished to make informal excursions in public, she should be allowed to do so,

On Sunday, 13 December, the Queen became a victim of the blizzards that swept across England but the Prince and Princess of Wales escaped the weather and travelled from Gloucestershire to London to attend a Christmas party at the Royal Opera House, Covent Garden.

The Princess accompanied her husband and the royal family to a service in St George's Chapel, Windsor, on Christmas morning. She wore a bright turquoise wool coat and dress designed by Bellville Sassoon with a matching hat by John Boyd.

free of scrutiny, and not feel 'beleaguered'. No demands were made by the Palace and no decisions were collectively taken by the editors, who were then invited to take sherry with the Queen herself and discuss the matter further. Her concern and deep affection for her daughter-in-law were very evident.

The following Friday the Princess paid a private visit to London, where she saw her gynaecologist, Mr Pinker, chose some new clothes and had lunch with her friends, Vicky Wilson and Kay Seth-Smith at the Young England Kindergarten.

On Sunday, *13 December*, she and the Prince attended a packed Communion Service in Gloucester Cathedral. Later that day the couple went to the Friends of Covent Garden's Christmas party at the Royal Opera House in London. This was the day on which the Queen, returning to London after visiting her daughter-in-law at Highgrove – for the fourth time in two months – and her daughter, Princess Anne, at Gatcombe Park, was delayed by blizzards and impassable roads which forced her to seek temporary and unexpected shelter at an inn, the Cross Hands Hotel, in Old Sodbury.

As a prelude to Christmas with the royal family, the Princess and her husband joined his father, sister, youngest brother, Prince Edward, and their labradors, for a long weekend at Balmoral, during which, it is believed, Prince Philip chaired a family 'pow-wow' about the family's image, performance and engagements over the past year and previewed the next. He himself had fulfilled 303 official engagements in 1981 and made eleven overseas trips.

The royal children flew with their father to Balmoral on Thursday, *17 December* and returned to London the following Monday. That evening the Prince and Princess of Wales went to Guildford Cathedral in snowy Surrey for an inter-denominational Christmas celebration and service.

On *23 December*, the entire royal family gathered at Windsor Castle for a five-day Christmas celebration of their own, during which they attended a service at St George's Chapel on Christmas Day.

Most of them then reassembled at Sandringham on *28 December* for their traditional New Year holiday. This year they were untroubled by ubiquitous press-

LEFT: *The new year brought a visit to Brixton for the Princess when on 23 January she opened a fair at the Dick Sheppard School. Proceeds were to help send pupils to Zimbabwe to study social conditions.*
BELOW: *Frances Shand Kydd with her second husband, Peter, on their sheep and cattle property at Yass, New South Wales, in March 1982. The bulls in the background are Pedigree Polled Shorthorns. The Shand Kydds' sheep won the Champion Wool Fleece and the Grand Champion Fleece awards at the Sydney Royal Easter Show in April 1982.*

men. The major upset of the holiday occurred when the Princess slipped and fell part of the way down a staircase in Sandringham. She was immediately put to bed and Prince Charles sat with her until a local doctor arrived. An examination established that neither the Princess nor her baby had been injured. This was confirmed when she was seen by Mr Pinker. Various tests, including an ultra-sound scan, revealed she was not carrying twins, as some had hoped. But neither she nor the Prince wished to know the sex of the baby revealed in an amniocentesis test.

The Princess was back at Althorp on Friday, *15 January*, for a party given by her father, Earl Spencer, for two hundred tenants, farmers, estate workers and their wives, most of whom had not been able to attend the wedding. Then, on *19 January*, when Prince Charles made a tour of Wales by helicopter, dropping in on snow-bound and flooded areas stricken by the worst winter weather for forty years, details of a new coat of arms for the Prince and Princess were announced. Approved by the couple and the Queen, and designed by the College of Arms, the new device will feature on flags flown over Highgrove when the royal couple are in residence, on their cars and on certain household effects.

Their first public engagement in 1982, on Saturday, *23 January*, was a visit to the Dick Sheppard School, a mixed comprehensive in Tulse Hill, South London, not far from the scene of the Brixton riots the previous summer. A bring-and-buy winter fair had been organized by the school to raise funds to send sixteen black and white pupils to Zimbabwe, to see how blacks and whites could work together there. The Princess bought three tombola tickets for 25 pence and won a set of plastic forks and spoons; the Prince won nothing, however, for his 50 pence. They guessed the weight of a large homemade cake, and the Princess paid 50 pence, borrowed from a bodyguard, for a raffle ticket for a suede coat.

Prince Charles's concern for racial harmony and his interest in minority groups was further reflected at the end of the month when it was disclosed that a British girl of West Indian origin, called Sonia, had been working as a secretary in his Palace office since 1980.

At the end of January, Mrs Shand Kydd and her husband, Peter, flew to Australia for two months, staying on their sheep and cattle properties at Yass in New South Wales. Mrs Shand Kydd was recovering from a gall-bladder operation. Far from well, she had lost over a stone in weight. She returned to Britain with her husband at the end of March, fully restored in health and strength.

On Tuesday, *2 February*, it was announced by the Palace that the Princess had agreed to become patron of four charities: the Pre-School Playgroups Association; the Malcolm Sargent Cancer Fund for Children; the Royal School for the Blind; the Welsh National Opera Company; and president of the Albany, a community centre in Deptford, South London, which is concerned with children at risk.

That evening she and the Prince attended a dinner in connection with the British Film Institute at 11 Downing Street. At the weekend the couple stayed at Eaton Hall, near Chester, home of the Duke and Duchess of Westminster. The Princess was godmother at the christening of her hosts' second child, Lady Edwina Louise Grosvenor; the Prince went hunting with the Cheshire Hunt.

At Sandringham, *6 February* – the thirtieth anniversary of the Queen's accession on the death of her father, George VI, at Sandringham – was spent quietly by the Queen and Prince Philip, although it was a significant date in her reign.

Five days later the Princess paid a surprise visit to the studios of ITN in Wells Street, London, where she met the duty newscasters and the team engaged on the preparation and transmission of the News at 5.45 p.m.

Within a week the Princess was once again front-page news herself. On Tuesday, *16 February*, she and the Prince, accompanied by Lord and Lady Romsey,

a police officer and two of their staff, flew on British Airways Flight 263 from Heathrow for a ten-day holiday in the Bahamas. Hoping to travel incognito, they had booked their £1,388 first class tickets in the names of Mr and Mrs Hardy. But their departure was known about in Fleet Street more than a month before it happened and revealed in the press a week before. At Heathrow the Princess, unwilling to accept all the press attention, averted her face from the cameras and without a smile or a wave hurried up the steps into the Tri-Star jet.

During the flight across the Atlantic, the royal party was served Buck's Fizz, a gourmet lunch, and later, high tea. They were attended by stewardesses who were also qualified nurses, trained in midwifery. British Airways also took the precaution of subjecting all the other passengers on the plane to a full security check. There was a stop-over at Hamilton, Bermuda, where the couple stretched their legs and went on a brief walkabout in the town; and at Nassau, they were met by the Governor-General of the Bahamas before flying on to the overgrown island of Eleuthera and their final destination, an even wilder, narrower island called Windermere.

RIGHT: *Shortly after their holiday in the West Indies the royal couple attended a service in Westminster Abbey to celebrate the centenary of the Royal College of Music. The Princess wore a velour coat designed by Bellville Sassoon and a matching hat by John Boyd.*
BELOW: *The Princess attended a charity preview of* The Little Foxes *which starred Elizabeth Taylor on 8 March, Miss Taylor said the Princess was 'charming, gracious and beautiful. I was more than thrilled to meet her.' Bellville Sassoon designed the white georgette evening dress worn by the Princess.*

Here, overlooking white sands, blue seas and tropical undergrowth, is a rambling, white-walled four-bed-roomed villa called Provender, which belongs to Countess Mountbatten, Earl Mountbatten's eldest daughter. Prince Charles first visited the island ten years ago as the Earl's guest – it is one of his favourite places – and he had wanted to share its idyllic pleasures with his wife.

The following morning the couple sunbathed and swam with the Romseys – the five-months' pregnant Princess wearing a cerise bikini. Across Cotton Bay, hidden in the undergrowth, were two sweating photographers, from *The Sun* and *Daily Star*, and two reporters. The resulting spread of fuzzy pictures, published in both papers on *18 February* and sold for large sums around the world, produced an outburst of condemnation and an excess of press hypocrisy and humbug. Michael Shea said, 'Such tasteless behaviour is in breach of normally accepted British press standards in respect of the privacy of the individuals.'

The next day, both the offending newspapers, richer and with more readers because of their scoops, printed apologies – but in its first editions *The Sun* reprinted the pictures. 'This is just what one would expect from *The Sun*,' said Michael Shea. Both papers were later condemned by the Press Council for their actions. Although the Princess was mortified by being thus publicly exposed, she apparently viewed the incident with some of her husband's resigned stoicism and was not unduly distressed.

Yet when the couple returned to England on Saturday, *27 February*, looking fit and tanned, the Princess was still disinclined to smile for photographers. Nor did she do so when she arrived at Westminster Abbey on Sunday afternoon for a Service of Thanksgiving marking the centenary of the Royal College of Music. A damp and dismal day was, however, lightened by the Queen Mother's generous and gentle smile. But the following Tuesday the Princess, much more relaxed and chic in a candy pink coat and hat, beamed happily among friends at the wedding in Otterbourne, Hampshire, of a schoolfriend, Diana Chamberlayne-Macdonald and James Lindsay-Bethune, aged twenty-six, only son of the heir to the Earl of Lindsay.

Her composure, confidence and cheerfulness were, however, evidently fully restored on *4* and *8 March*: when with the Prince she attended a star-studded charity gala at the newly opened multi-million pound Barbican Arts and Conference Centre in the City of London; and when at the Victoria Palace Theatre she met another of the world's most famous women,

A guard of honour was mounted outside the Victoria Palace Theatre when the Princess of Wales left after a performance of The Little Foxes *on 8 March.*

actress Elizabeth Taylor, after a charity preview of *The Little Foxes*.

A third evening event followed on Sunday, *14 March*, when the Princess and her husband – he as President of the Royal College of Music Appeals Committee – went to the Royal Albert Hall to hear a performance of Berlioz's *Grande Messe des Morts* sung by the Bach Choir, of which the Prince is patron and with whom he used to sing himself. On this occasion the royal family were represented in the choir by the Duchess of Kent. The choir sang at the Prince and Princess's wedding.

LEFT: *The Prince of Wales as patron of the Bach Choir was accompanied by his wife to a performance of Berlioz's* Grande Messe des Morts *in the Royal Albert Hall on 14 March 1982. Under a velvet cape she chose a red chiffon evening dress flecked with gold designed by Bellville Sassoon.*
BELOW: *It was a cold day for the Cheltenham Gold Cup Race Meeting on 18 March. Ruth, Lady Fermoy, in attendance on the Queen Mother, watched the races with her grand-daughter and the Prince of Wales.*

By now the Princess's official engagements were becoming fewer. On *16 March*, looking very cheerful, she attended the banquet given by the Queen for the Sultan of Oman, who was on a State Visit to Britain. Two days later, at the Cheltenham Gold Cup Race meeting, she watched the races with Prince Charles and the Queen Mother from the royal box. The following Monday, *22 March*, the Prince and Princess flew north in an Andover of the Queen's Flight, piloted by the Prince. They visited St Patrick's Centre in Huddersfield and another youth centre in Newcastle upon Tyne, where she tried her hand at playing darts, met a punk pop-group, went on a walkabout and helped to save a small boy caught by a fallen barrier. Then, on *30 March*, the royal couple travelled in the Royal Train to Leeds, where that morning they opened an extension of St Gemma's Hospice, a home for thirty-eight terminally ill people. One 74-year-old patient, Edwin Wilson, became headline news himself when he told the staff of the hospital what the Princess had said on hearing that he and the Duke of Edinburgh shared the same birthday, 10 June, and that it would be all right he thought if the baby was born also on that day. 'It's

ABOVE: *The Prince and Princess visited St Patrick's Youth Centre in Huddersfield on 22 March 1982.*
RIGHT: *After the Princess visited St Gemma's Hospital in Leeds on 29 March, one of the patients said she had told him her baby was due on her twenty-first birthday, 1 July. That day she wore a sailor hat trimmed with velvet, designed by John Boyd, and a matching coat from Bellville Sassoon.*
LEFT: *On 2 April the Prince and Princess opened the new Chinese Community Centre in Henry Street, Liverpool, during their visit to Merseyside.*

not due then,' said the Princess with a laugh, 'it's due on *my* birthday, 1 July!'

After this visit she returned in the Royal Train to London, while the Prince drove to York, where he opened the 'Vikings in England' Exhibition.

Four days later, the couple attended another opening, that of a pagoda-style cultural centre for the large Chinese community in Liverpool. Prince Charles, who had earlier visited Toxteth and Radio Merseyside, arrived before his young wife at 12.15. Half an hour later, as his young wife passed down the row of dignitaries who were being presented to her, she was so absorbed she failed to notice her husband had joined the end of the line – until he grasped her automatically

The royal couple shared a joke with Mrs Nicholas Gaselee at the Grand National Meeting at Aintree on Saturday, 3 April 1982. Nick Gaselee is the Prince's trainer; his home, and the stables for the Prince's horses, are at Upper Lambourn in Berkshire.

outstretched hand and said, 'We've met before, I think.' Then he kissed her cheek. Taken unawares, she blushed.

The following day, Saturday, *3 April*, the couple paid a private visit to the Aintree Racecourse near Liverpool to watch the Grand National. Again the Prince arrived first, and walked the course, inspecting the jumps – his former steeplechaser, Good Prospect, was running in the National. The Princess arrived in time for a snack lunch in the royal box, and then with the Prince, Nick Gaselee (the Prince's horse trainer) and Mrs Gaselee she watched two races from the grandstand before driving in a Range Rover to the end of the course near Becher's Brook and the Canal Turn. From there they watched the Grand National being run. At one point the pregnant Princess and Mrs Gaselee climbed onto the Range Rover's bonnet to get a better view. Grittar, backed by the Prince, won at 7–1; Good Prospect was pulled up at the seventeenth fence.

The Princess was back in Wales on *7 April*, when she opened a £10-million extension of the Sony factory at Bridgend, Mid Glamorgan. She was flown there by

helicopter from Highgrove. It was a very windy morning and at one point she nearly lost her hat. Before she toured the factory she donned a protective baseball cap and glasses, and afterwards she was presented with cassette players and a book on childcare by a Japanese co-founder of the Sony firm. This time, in making her obligatory speech, she spoke slowly and with some expression. As in all her visits she made a special point of talking to children. This was scheduled to have been her last official and solo engagement before the birth of her first child; a week later, however, it was announced that she had agreed to fulfill an engagement on behalf of the Queen Mother in Deptford on 18 May, five weeks or so before the baby was due.

The Easter weekend was spent by the Prince and Princess at Highgrove – although on Easter Monday they paid a family visit to Windsor Castle. On the Sunday, at very short notice, they arrived at St Mary's Church in Tetbury to take their first communion service there together. The pleasant surprise of their appearance in the church was outweighed by the disappointment of the vast crowds (and the horde of pressmen) who invaded the Badminton Horse Trials the following week (14–18 April), expecting to see the royal pair. In the royal box they saw instead the Queen Mother and Prince Edward, who were watching Princess Anne and her husband competing in the Three-Day Event – the

ABOVE: *It was a windy day on 7 April when the Princess of Wales opened the new Picture Tube Plant of Sony Limited at Bridgend in Mid Glamorgan. Both the Princess and her lady-in-waiting, Hazel West, had difficulty keeping their hats on.*

BELOW: *The royal couple, as Duke and Duchess of Cornwall, began a three-day visit to the Duchy's possessions in the Isles of Scilly on 20 April 1982. Prince Charles piloted their helicopter from Highgrove to the island of St Mary's where the couple were welcomed by John Higgs, the Duchy of Cornwall Secretary, and his wife.*

Princess fell at The Lake. That Saturday, the Princess of Wales went shopping in Tetbury, apparently looking for a birthday card for Lady Sarah Armstrong-Jones, who would be eighteen on 1 May – or for Lady Helen Windsor, the Duchess of Kent's only daughter, also eighteen on 28 April; or for Princess Michael's daughter, Lady Gabriella, who was one on 23 April.

On Sunday, *18 April*, it was stated in *The Observer*: 'The Princess has had a routine medical scan to monitor the growth and condition of the baby – and the pictures . . . showed that the healthy baby is a boy.' This was taken up by other newspapers – Buckingham Palace refused to comment. The papers' representatives, excited by this speculation and frustrated by the royal couple's non-appearance at Badminton, turned up in force on the Isles of Scilly on Tuesday, *20 April*. The Prince and Princess, as Duke and Duchess of Cornwall, were making what was described by a Duchy of Cornwall official as 'a private working visit' to their most romantic, sea-girt possessions off Land's End.

Their visit coincided with the public showing in London of a highly romanticized portrait of the Princess commissioned by Prince Charles. It was painted by Susan Ryder, aged thirty-eight, who responded to criticisms that the Princess looked as if she had been 'dropped in a puddle of ice cream' or was sitting in the middle of 'her entire Monday morning wash' by saying

LEFT: *A few hours after arriving on St Mary's, the Princess met some of the many children who had gathered to welcome the royal couple to the islands.*
RIGHT: *On the evening of her first day on St Mary's, the Princess wore a blue and white spotted dress for a Reception held in the Town Hall in Hugh Town, not far from the Duchy's bungalow, Tamarisk, where the couple stayed during their visit.*
BELOW: *At the Hugh Town quay, the Princess was helped aboard the Dorrien-Smiths' launch, Mellegdan, to join them and the Prince for lunch at Tresco Abbey on Wednesday, 21 April.*

'I know it's not realistic . . . but the Princess has a marvellous, glamorous personality.'

Although the three-day royal visit to the Isles of Scilly, the Princess's first, was not 'official', security precautions were more than routine, and on these small islands more evident than on the mainland. Special Branch and Cornish policemen, as well as sniffer-dogs, bomb disposal men and divers (there to prevent any royal boat being sabotaged) were to be seen in the narrow streets checking both people and properties. The dogs, trained to detect explosives, were taken over every place an hour before the royal couple's expected arrival, and throughout the visit a helicopter and a medical team were on standby in case of any emergency.

The Prince and Princess flew from Highgrove by helicopter to St Mary's airport, from where they drove

straight to Tamarisk, the royal bungalow behind the Duchy of Cornwall's offices, over which the Duchy's standard (not the Prince's) flew. Later that afternoon they drove in a Land-Rover to the village green at the centre of Hugh Town and went on a twenty-minute walkabout among a delighted crowd of holidaymakers and islanders, whose children presented the Princess with a total of seventy-four posies and bunches of flowers. At one point she ducked under a rope barrier to talk to some pensioners. From here the couple walked to the Town Hall, for a Reception given by the Council at 6 p.m. The Princess was cheerful, but seemed tired.

The following misty morning, the Prince visited the islands of St Agnes and Bryher on the Duchy launch, *Dolphin*, before going to Tresco, where he was joined by the Princess. The couple had lunch in Tresco Abbey, the home of thirty-year-old Robert Dorrien-Smith, and his wife, Lady Emma. Afterwards the royal guests were shown around the luxuriant Abbey Gardens, full of

The Prince of Wales, Duke of Cornwall, admired a baby girl as he and his wife left the Audit Lunch held for his Duchy tenants on 22 April in the Sunset Restaurant on the main quay of St Mary's.

exotic plants and flowers, some of which had been cut to decorate Tamarisk the evening before. The 1,000 acres of the island of Tresco, with all the uninhabited islands and rocky islets, were leased to the Dorrien-Smiths by the Duchy for ninety-nine years in 1929.

At about 3.30 p.m. the royal couple returned to St Mary's in the Dorrien-Smiths' motor-cruiser, *Mellegdan*. That evening the Prince went for a run in the Duchy speedboat, *Imelda*, named after the wife of President Marcos of the Philippines, whose gift it was.

On Thursday, *22 April*, the Audit Lunch held annually by the Duchy of Cornwall for its tenants was hosted in the Sunset Restaurant on the quay by the Duke and Duchess themselves. After lunch the Duchess (who had been prophetically nicknamed as such by friends when she lived in London), talked to some of the restaurant's staff. On seeing a baby in its mother's arms she exclaimed, 'Oh, the joy of things to come!' She and the Duke returned to Tamarisk in a Land-Rover and that afternoon he visited the last of the inhabited islands, St Martin's, without his wife, travelling thither in *Mellegdan*.

The couple left the Isles of Scilly at 9.30 on Friday morning, flying to Highgrove in a helicopter of the Queen's Flight and escorted by a Royal Navy helicopter from Culdrose. They were involved in more Duchy matters the following Monday when they attended an Audit Dinner at the Carlyon Bay Hotel, St Austell.

After this the Princess settled down to await the birth of her baby. Continuing sickness and discomfort had bedevilled every month of her pregnancy and she now had to take things easy. But this period of necessary rest and inactivity was interrupted by the move into her next new home, in Kensington Palace, on 14 May, and by her last official engagement before she became a mother. In the meantime, she sometimes accompanied her husband to his polo matches.

On Sunday, *2 May*, the Princess drove Prince Charles to the Guards' Polo Club at Smith's Lawn, Windsor Great Park where he played polo for Pegasus – his first polo match of the season. It was a chilly, windy day and for most of the match the Princess watched from their Ford Granada estate car, chatting with her bodyguards and the Prince's Argentinian groom, Raoul Correa. Later she drove her husband home to Highgrove.

The weekend after she and the Prince moved into their Kensington Palace apartments, they were the guests of Lord and Lady Romsey at Broadlands. On Saturday, *15 May* the Princess watched her husband play polo for the Foresters in the Lord Mountbatten Memorial match at the New Park Farm ground near Brockenhurst. But on the Sunday she was absent when he played in polo matches, at Ham and Smith's Lawn.

The Princess's last official public engagement was on Tuesday, *18 May*, when she opened the new £2.8 million

ABOVE: *On 2 May, the Princess watched her husband play polo for Pegasus at Smith's Lawn, Windsor. She wore an Australian wool jersey, one of a pair given to the couple as a wedding present by Kim Wran, daughter of the New South Wales premier.*
RIGHT: *The Princess's last official engagement before the birth of her baby was on 18 May at Deptford, where she opened the new Albany Community Centre.*

Albany Community Centre at Deptford in southeast London. It was a warm and humid morning, and the Princess, although she looked well, seemed to tire easily. She often sat on chairs or tables to talk to people as she toured the Centre for over an hour, visiting a crèche, a pensioners' bingo session and talking to parents and children in a restaurant. She told one woman that Prince Charles was reading books about pregnancy, babies and childcare. 'He keeps telling me what I should be doing,' she said. To other enquiries about her baby she replied, 'I hope it's a boy. But we'll have to wait and see.'

This final engagement before the birth was the first concerning the Princess to be recorded in the Court Circular under the heading *Kensington Palace*. It was in her new home, where she now had the pleasure of

ABOVE: *On 12 June, after the Trooping the Colour, the Queen, the Princess and other members of the royal family watched a fly past from the balcony of Buckingham Palace.*
LEFT: *While the Princess watched her husband play polo at Smith's Lawn, Windsor, on 4 June, she remarked to photographer, Tim Graham, 'You and your friends rather spoil the game for me, and I absolutely love polo.' This was said without any rancour, and later, concerned as ever about people's feelings, she asked her detective to assure Graham the remark was not meant personally.*

entertaining close female friends and her family, that the Princess spent the last weeks of her pregnancy. The Prince was often absent fulfilling engagements and playing polo. But most of his engagements were during the evening and in the London area, and when he was not obliged to attend some military or business dinner, he stayed at home with his wife. They also spent their weekends quietly when she occasionally travelled with him to polo grounds or visited friends.

The summer is always the royal family's busiest time. Besides a crowded round of engagements, there were in June such annual court and social events as the Queen's Birthday Parade and Trooping the Colour (on *12 June*) and the Order of the Garter Service at St George's Chapel, Windsor (*14 June*), which were followed by Royal Ascot week. These events were preceded this year by the three-day visit (*7–9 June*) of President

ABOVE: *The Princess was with the royal family again at Royal Ascot on Tuesday, 15 June, the day the Argentine forces surrendered to the British in the Falklands.*
LEFT: *After the Prince's team,* Les Diables Bleus, *lost in the final of the Queen's Cup Tournament at Smith's Lawn on Sunday, 6 June, the Princess carried the trophy, presented to him by the Queen, back to the car.*

Reagan and his wife – they stayed at Windsor Castle. The Princess met the President but did not attend the banquet given in his honour on Tuesday, *8 June*. That day she privately visited a kindergarten in Caterham, Surrey, and met wives and children of men serving with the Welsh Guards, whose 1st Battalion suffered heavy casualties the same day in the Falklands. June 1982 was also a time of great historical and national events: the visit of Pope John Paul II to England, Scotland and Wales, and the ten-week war in the Falkland Islands, where the Queen's second son, Prince Andrew, served as a helicopter pilot on HMS *Invincible*.

It was also a month for royal birthdays: the 51st birthday of Prince Philip on *10 June*, that of the young Duchess of Gloucester ten days later, and the twentieth birthday of the Earl of St Andrews, the Kents' eldest son, on *26 June*. But two other birthdays would be more keenly anticipated than any other that month, by the royal family and the media: the Princess's own 21st birthday on *1 July* – and that of her first child.

CHAPTER TWELVE

Birthday

THE CHILD WAS BORN on Monday, 21 June 1982, at 9.03 p.m., just before sunset on the longest day of the year and three days before Midsummer's Day.

It was also the first day of the Lawn Tennis Championships at Wimbledon and the day on which England's football team entered the second phase of the World Cup in Spain – only to be knocked out later. The weather that day in London was cloudy with occasional rain. That night there was a new moon.

Two days earlier, Prince Charles had played polo at Windsor. His team was beaten 7–3 in the final of the Mountbatten Cup; the Queen presented him with a runners' up medal. The Princess was at Highgrove.

The next morning, on Sunday (Father's Day), the Prince, accompanied by Francis Cornish and Major Winter, flew from Highgrove in a Wessex helicopter of the Queen's Flight to northern France, where he was welcomed by President Mitterand. Prince Charles, wearing the uniform of the Parachute Regiment's Colonel-in-Chief, reviewed the French and British troops. He also made a speech in which he praised the

2nd Parachute Regiment's exploits in World War II and more recently in the South Atlantic.

Four hours after his arrival in France, the Prince flew back to England, to Windsor Castle. And he drove on to Kensington Palace to join the Princess. There, that evening, preparing herself for the birth of her child, she had her hair done by Kevin Shanley. The birth was now imminent, having apparently been expected in late June – but not, as the papers had surmised, on 1 July. Another newspaper misconception was an alleged dispute between the Queen and her daughter-in-law about the baby's birthplace: there was never any question about it being born in Buckingham Palace. Kensington Palace, the parents' home, was considered for a while, but medical advice and the Princess's inclination was to have the child in the private Lindo Wing of St Mary's Hospital, Paddington.

Just before dawn on Monday morning, the Princess experienced the first signs of early labour, and having woken her husband, she dressed and was driven with him in a Rover police car through the deserted streets of West London to the hospital. They arrived at 5.10 a.m. and she was taken in a lift to a private room on the fourth floor.

The 54-bed Lindo Wing, built out of a £115,000 donation from a landowner, Frank Lindo, to St Mary's Hospital, is a featureless building tacked onto the side of St Mary's in South Wharf Road; it was opened by the Queen Mother in 1937. Its interior is spartan, and the private rooms, twelve feet square, hardly reflect their high price of £126.90 a day. The food is varied but plainly cooked. The Princess's room, pink-coloured with blue and beige floral wallpaper behind the bed, was uncarpeted, apart from a mat under the washbasin.

LEFT: *The Princess continued to appear in public throughout her pregnancy. This last picture taken of her and her husband before the birth shows them at Smith's Lawn, Windsor – six days before their son was born.*
RIGHT: *Prince William of Wales made his first public appearance on Tuesday, 22 June, when the Princess of Wales left hospital exactly twenty-one hours after his birth.*

Mr George Pinker, the Princess's gynaecologist, is married to a former nurse and has four children of his own, including 27-year-old twins.

Throughout Monday, 21 June, bunches of flowers continued to arrive at the Lindo Wing where the Princess was having her baby.

There was no bathroom *en suite* but such facilities were opposite her room. Furnishings, apart from the metal-frame bed, included a small teak wardrobe and dressing-table, a television set, a telephone, an arm-chair, a bedside locker, bed-table and some upright chairs. But the unfussy care and relaxed but clockwork efficiency of the Lindo Wing are first class.

Seven royal babies have already been delivered there by Mr George Pinker, the Queen's Surgeon-Gynaecologist since 1973, the first being the Duchess of Glouces-ter's eldest child, the Earl of Ulster, who was born in October 1974. Her two daughters, Lady Davina and Lady Rose, were also born in the Lindo Wing (in 1977 and 1980), as were Princess Michael of Kent's two children, Lord Frederick and Lady Gabriella (in 1979 and 1981), and the son and daughter of Princess Anne, Peter and Zara Phillips (in 1977 and 1981).

Mr Pinker qualified at St Mary's Hospital in 1947 and has been consultant gynaecologist and obstetrician there since 1958; he holds the same position at four

other London hospitals. A handsome, kindly, grey-haired man, now fifty-seven, he seldom wears a hospital coat when attending a birth, merely putting on a plastic apron, a pair of rubber overboots, and rolling up his sleeves. His view is that birth is a natural process and should be treated as such. He likes the father to attend. 'I think it helps the mother,' he says. 'I also believe it strengthens family bonds.'

After the Princess's arrival, Prince Charles hardly left his wife's room as the spasms of her labour came and went. He would be the first heir to the throne to witness the birth of his own first child – although Prince Albert had attended the birth of Queen Victoria's first baby, a daughter, in November 1840. The Prince of Wales sat beside his wife at the head of her bed, keeping out of the way of the midwife and anaesthetist, who observed both the Princess and the equipment assessing her condition. A drip machine, entonox machine and an incubator stood by in case of emergencies. It is likely that facilities for foetal heart monitoring, and also an epidural anaesthetic or pethidine injections would have been available according to the patient's needs. As the day progressed and her contractions increased, she was constantly watched and attended, chiefly by Mr Pinker and the midwife, Sister Delphine Stevens. The baby was eventually born during the evening after a thirteen-hour labour (about average for a first child), while Prince Charles held his young wife's hand.

It was a boy. He 'cried lustily' at birth, and was probably handed to his mother before the umbilical cord was cut. This is the hospital's practice – as is putting the baby immediately to the breast to feed. After being washed and weighed – he was 7lb 1½oz – the baby was given, wrapped in a towel, to his mother. Plastic identity tags were later attached to his ankle and wrist bearing the legend *Baby Wales*.

Celebrations began and joyful telephone calls were made, informing both families and the nation of the birth of a son to the Prince and Princess of Wales, the first child born to parents with that title since 1905. He would be second in line of succession to the throne, after his father, and displace his uncles, Prince Andrew and Prince Edward, and his aunt, Princess Anne.

According to Debrett, the baby Prince is the most English heir to the throne to be born for more than 400 years, being 39⅜ per cent English, 15⅝ per cent Scottish, 6¼ per cent Irish and 6½ per cent American. He is also of Greek, Danish and German blood through his grandparents, the Queen and the Duke of Edinburgh. Prince Charles himself is only 18¾ per cent English. He himself was born in Buckingham Palace. His mother, the Queen, is the only monarch in the twentieth century not to have been born in a royal residence. She was born in 1926 at 17 Bruton Street, off New Bond Street in London, the home of her parents, then Duke and Duchess of York.

The latest royal baby's birth was not the swiftest to follow a royal wedding: Queen Victoria bore her first child just over nine months after her marriage in February 1840; her first son's wife, Princess Alexandra of Denmark, had her first child prematurely ten months after her wedding; and the Queen gave birth to Prince Charles six days before her first wedding anniversary. Mrs Shand Kydd, the Princess's mother, bore her first child, Sarah, nine months after her wedding and a few months after her nineteenth birthday.

The official announcement of the new baby's birth was displayed at the gates of Buckingham Palace at 10.25 p.m. It read:

Her Royal Highness the Princess of Wales was today safely delivered of a son at 9.03 p.m. Her Royal Highness and her child are both doing well.

The baby is the Queen's third grandchild. When he was born she was at Buckingham Palace; Prince Philip was dining at St John's College, Cambridge; the baby's great-aunt, Princess Margaret, was at the theatre, watching a performance of *Song and Dance*. His aunt, Princess Anne, was in New Mexico – 'Oh, good,' she said when told the news. The baby's uncles, Prince Andrew and Prince Edward, were, respectively, at sea off the Falkland Islands and at school at Gordonstoun. His other grandparents, Mrs Shand Kydd and Earl Spencer, were at their respective London homes. Mrs Shand Kydd had travelled from Scotland on the Sunday for the start of the Wimbledon fortnight. The Princess's grandmother, Lady Fermoy, was at a dinner-party, where she was telephoned by her daughter with the news, and the Queen Mother was at Clarence House.

Outside the Lindo Wing, news of the birth reached the crowds through transistor radios broadcasting the 10 o'clock news. 'It's a boy! It's a *boy*!' they shouted, and broke into choruses of 'For he's a jolly good fellow!' and 'Rule Britannia!' 'We want Charlie! – Nice one, Charlie!' they chanted like a soccer crowd.

In Grosvenor Square, Earl Spencer emerged to be questioned by television reporters and the press. The Prince, he said, had telephoned him. 'He's over the moon,' said the Earl. 'Absolutely over the moon . . . It's a very historic occasion, and I'm happy to be part of it. Prince Charles told me Diana was absolutely wonderful. I think it's a very lucky baby to have a mother like Diana. I'm so proud of her. It's been a worrying day . . . Now I'm going to have a beer.'

At 11.00 p.m. a blue Ford Granada drove up South Wharf Road and halted at the hospital steps. A few minutes later, the Prince's personal detective and friend, John MacLean, appeared, soon followed in a blaze of television lights by the beaming Prince himself.

The official announcement of the Prince's birth displayed outside Buckingham Palace. This was signed by Dr John Batten, head of the Queen's medical household, by the anaesthetist, Dr Clive Roberts, by the paediatrician, Dr David Harvey, and by Mr Pinker.

ABOVE: *The Princess of Wales' grandmother, Ruth, Lady Fermoy at her flat in Belgravia, London. Lady Fermoy studied the piano at the Paris Conservatoire under Alfred Cortot. In 1931 she married Maurice, the 4th Baron Fermoy. After his death in 1956 she was appointed Woman of the Bedchamber to the Queen Mother.*
BELOW: *Prince Charles waves proudly to the crowds as he leaves the hospital after his son's birth.*

He stopped to wave at jubilant crowds, now numbering about five hundred. Some people, led by reporters and photographers, dived forward eager to congratulate the new father and shake his hand. 'Thank you, thank you,' he said. For several minutes he was happily mobbed as the police in the street seemed bemused.

Answering a barrage of questions, the Prince replied, 'I'm obviously relieved and delighted – thirteen hours is a long time to wait . . . It's rather a grown-up thing I find – it's rather a shock to the system.' How was the baby ? 'He looks marvellous – fair, sort of blondish . . . He's not bad.' Was the baby like him ? 'I've no idea. It's a bit difficult to tell at the moment.' Asked about the baby's names, he said, 'We've thought of one or two. There's a bit of an argument about it, but we'll and one eventually.'

A girl seized and kissed him. The crowd sang – 'Nice one, Charlie!' 'Give us another one!'

The Prince smiling merrily retorted, 'Bloody hell! Give us a chance. You ask my wife – I don't think she'd be too pleased just yet. Sorry you've had to wait so long.' As detectives struggled to open a car door for him, he called out, 'Now, can someone ask them not to make too much noise when I've gone, as some sleep is needed ?' After he was driven away the celebrating crowds began to disperse.

ABOVE LEFT: *After visiting the Princess with Lady Jane Fellowes, Mrs Shand Kydd returned to Scotland on a British Airways Shuttle service. At her request everybody on board toasted her new grandson's health in champagne.*
ABOVE RIGHT: *The Queen was greeted in the hospital foyer by Prince Charles who kissed her on both cheeks.*
RIGHT: *Earl Spencer said after he visited the hospital, 'Lovely baby . . . Not a little puckered up face at all . . . Beautiful baby.'*

They were back the following morning ready to hail every new visitor to the Lindo Wing, which was inundated with flowers for the Princess. The Prince arrived at 8.45 a.m. He was asked how he was feeling. 'I'm very well. Thank you very much,' he replied. Did he sleep well? 'Yes thanks – I'm going to find out how things are now.'

Mrs Shand Kydd and her second daughter, Lady Jane Fellowes, arrived at 9.22. When she left, Mrs Shand Kydd crossed the street and spoke to reporters behind the barricade. 'My grandson is everything his father said last night. He's a lovely baby . . . The Princess looked radiant, absolutely radiant . . . There's a lot of happiness up there.' After her visit Mrs Shand Kydd returned to Scotland at lunch time.

At 10.52 the Queen arrived and stayed at the hospital for twenty minutes. Her visit was followed by that of the Princess's father, Earl Spencer. The Queen Mother, on a visit to County Durham, said: 'It's a lovely, happy occasion.'

When the Prince left about midday he said of his wife, 'She's very well, thank you.' Of the baby he said, 'He's in excellent form too, thank goodness. Looking a bit more human this morning.'

As the Prince and Princess left the hospital neither responded to cries of – 'Show us the baby! Can we see his face?' They were both far more absorbed by their first-born.

In the meantime, messages of congratulation, which began arriving at Buckingham Palace after the birth was announced – seven hundred telegrams arrived overnight – continued to pour in from heads of state, foreign royal families, and commoners all over the world. Most of these messages were answered by Oliver Everett and Anne Beckwith-Smith. By the end of the day 1,800 gifts had also been received, including hundreds of handknitted baby clothes, adding to the thousands of woollen toys, layettes and clothes already accumulated at the Palace. When Prince Charles was born, 1½ tons of nappies were received.

At 1 o'clock an official 41 gun salute was fired in Hyde Park by the King's Troop, Royal Horse Artillery, and

by members of the Honourable Artillery Company at the Tower of London. At the same time, the bells of St Paul's Cathedral and Westminster Abbey were rung. But the Department of the Environment had made no provisions to floodlight the fountains in Trafalgar Square blue for a boy, as had been done on Prince Charles's birth.

Later that afternoon the Prince returned to the Lindo Wing. At 5 p.m. the Queen's Press Secretary, Michael Shea, appeared and told the astonished press that the couple would be leaving the hospital in an hour's time. Queried about the Princess's departure less than twenty-four hours after the birth, Mr Shea smiled and said, 'It's the fashionable thing to do!'

Such a short royal stay in hospital was unprecedented and even in ordinary circumstances exceptional, first-time mothers usually remaining in hospital for five days at least. But the medical back-up and care available to the Princess were also exceptional, and both she and the baby were in 'fine condition' according to Mr Pinker. When asked if she had had a natural child-birth, he said, 'Yes, it was – well almost. Just at the end the Princess did have a bit of pain relief. But I'm afraid I can't go into details.' He said he would be visiting Kensington Palace every day. In addition, mother and baby would be attended for over a month by a paedi-atric nurse, Miss Ann Wallace, aged forty-eight, who had cared for both of Princess Anne's babies. Miss Wallace would be replaced by Barbara Barnes at the end of July.

It was none the less with amazed delight that at 6.03 p.m. the crowd and pressmen greeted the emergence of the Prince and Princess of Wales from the Lindo Wing, with the Prince carrying his infant son.

For some moments the couple stood, receiving the plaudits of the crowd; the Princess blushed. Then Prince Charles carefully handed the sleeping baby, born to be King, to his wife. The people cheered.

Someone played 'Land of Hope and Glory' on a cassette-recorder as the couple entered the Prince's car, the Princess easing herself cautiously onto the back seat, the baby still in her arms. Having earlier been shown how to wash and dress him, she had removed her engagement ring, lest it scratch him. Now she held him close.

They were driven through rush-hour traffic, wor-sened by the Underground strike, to Kensington Palace, where members of the royal family who live there – Princess Margaret, her daughter and the Gloucesters – were waiting to welcome them home.

In the days that followed, the Princess breast-fed her baby. But such was her superb state of health, main-tained before the birth by antenatal exercises and sessions in the Buckingham Palace swimming-pool, that her figure very soon regained its natural trim

Prince William's nursery has furnishings bought by the Princess of Wales from Dragons, the baby boutique in Knightsbridge.

proportions. Contrary to royal custom, her baby son was probably not circumcized a few days after his birth – as his father had been (by a Jewish doctor). Meanwhile his parents discussed possible names and his mother was busy choosing baby clothes, some from Please Mum in New Bond Street – where romper suits cost about £65 and party clothes somewhat more. Much of her time was spent (when not with her baby) in trying to thank people for the thousands of letters, telegrams and gifts that had been sent, and in greeting those family visitors and friends who called at Kensington Palace to wish her well and see her child.

Prince Charles resumed his public engagements on Thursday, 24 June and he was soon back on the polo field, at Cowdray Park on the 25th and at Smith's Lawn two days later.

On Monday, 28 June, the week-old baby's names were announced by Buckingham Palace. They were William, Arthur, Philip, Louis. He would be known as Prince William of Wales.

That morning, Prince Charles visited Haslar Naval Hospital near Gosport to meet servicemen wounded in the Falklands War. During his visit, he was asked why he and his wife had chosen William. 'It's a very nice name,' he replied. 'And it's not a name that now exists in the immediate family.'

The last Prince William, son of the late Duke of Gloucester, was killed in an air-crash in 1972. The last King William was William IV, who died in 1837 and was succeeded by his niece, Queen Victoria. William I (1027–87), was otherwise known as the Conqueror, or the Bastard – which he was. His third son, William Rufus (1056–1100), became William II; and William III (1650–1702), became King because as Prince of Orange he had married Princess Mary, who succeeded her father James II in 1689.

Arthur is one of the names of both Prince Charles and his grandfather, George VI. Philip is the Prince's father's name, and Louis that of his great-uncle, Earl Mountbatten. The bookmakers' evens favourite, George, was not chosen, nor were Charles, James and John – nor Elvis, Bjorn and Canute, at 1000–1.

The names of the baby's six godparents were also announced by the Palace on 28 June. They were all chiefly friends of Prince Charles. The six were: ex-King Constantine of Greece, a sporting friend of the Prince; Lord Romsey, grandson of Earl Mountbatten; Sir Laurens van der Post, the 75-year-old South African writer; Princess Alexandra, cousin of Prince Charles; the Duchess of Westminster, aged twenty-three; and Lady Susan Hussey, aged forty-three, one of the Queen's most loyal ladies-in-waiting. Sir Laurens and his wife were guests of the Prince and Princess the previous October at Balmoral; the Prince was god-father to Lord Romsey's first child in November, and the Princess godmother to the Duchess of Westminster's second daughter. Only Lord Romsey had featured in press speculations about the list, which showed the parents' wide-ranging personal choice and the evident respect and liking they had for the six.

Another announcement, on 30 June, was that Prince Charles's equerry, Major Winter, had been promoted to Lieutenant Colonel and would take command of the 10th Battalion the Parachute Regiment in August. His place in the Prince's household would be taken by Major David Bromhead, aged thirty-eight, of the Royal Regiment of Wales.

On Thursday, 1 July, the Princess of Wales was twenty-one and her baby ten days old. She received over two thousand birthday cards and forty sacks of presents for her and Prince William. During the day

LEFT: *A portrait by Snowdon of Her Royal Highness The Princess of Wales on the occasion of her 21st birthday on 1 July 1982.*

As a tribute to the Princess of Wales, a set of four stamps was issued in sixteen British Commonwealth countries to commemorate her 21st birthday.

the Princess was visited by her mother as well as by her father and step-mother. In the morning Prince Charles paid his third visit to a military hospital to talk to servicemen injured in the Falklands War, but he was back at Kensington Palace in time for lunch with his wife. As the Queen, Prince Philip and their households were in Edinburgh on a week-long visit to Scotland, and the baby's uncles elsewhere, there was no full-scale royal celebration that night, just a small dinner-party for some close friends.

Prince Charles fulfilled altogether about a dozen engagements in July, while his wife stayed away from public view. However, on 26 July, five weeks after the baby's birth and three days before her wedding anniversary she attended the Falklands Service at St Paul's Cathedral with other members of the royal family.

On the morning of the anniversary, at Brize Norton, Prince Charles welcomed the Welsh Guards returning from the Falkland Islands. After lunching with his wife at home he played polo at Cowdray Park and that evening the royal couple dined at Kensington Palace. They spent the weekend at Highgrove.

The Princess's second royal year began with a celebration. On Wednesday, 4 August, the day before the Queen's household left for Scotland and Balmoral, the

ABOVE: *The Princess of Wales made her first public appearance since the birth of her son on Monday, 26 July, when she joined the royal family at St Paul's Cathedral for the Falkland Islands Service.*

royal family gathered at Buckingham Palace for the christening of the infant Prince. The date was a happy and thoughtful choice – it was the Queen Mother's 82nd birthday.

Tradition was for once fully observed by the baby's parents. The ceremony, attended by the six godparents, both families and a few friends, took place at noon in the mirrored splendour of the Music Room, where the infant's father, Prince Charles, had also been christened, as had other members of the family. Each baby wore the christening robe of white silk and Honiton lace originally made for Queen Victoria's first

LEFT: *This study by Snowdon of the Prince and Princess of Wales with their son, Prince William of Wales, was released on the royal couple's first wedding anniversary, 29 July 1982. The Princess wore a cream silk dress with a diamond and pearl necklace and matching heart-shaped diamond earrings.*

child. The Archbishop of Canterbury, Dr Runcie, baptized the baby prince at the silver gilt Lily Font. After the ceremony, the sixty guests had lunch in the State Dining-room at the Palace.

It was an occasion that may well be repeated within two years, and if the next child of the Prince and Princess of Wales follows the remarkably consistent pattern (of a boy first and then a girl) set by the Queen and repeated by every princess and royal duchess since, Prince William of Wales will be joined by a younger sister before too long – possibly even by twin girls. For there are four sets of twins (two identical) in the Princess's family, and two on the Queen Mother's side. As it is, astrologers predict that Prince William will have a dual personality, being both athletic and artistic, adventurous and home-loving, extrovert and shy. With Sagittarius rising and the Sun in Cancer, he should be closest, they say, to his mother in character and affection, and though doted on by his father, more in sympathy with his Uncle Andrew.

But who can say what really lies ahead, what will occur in the world before Prince William comes of age in the year 2000? Certainly the first royal year of the Princess of Wales brought her and her husband much happiness, establishing them and their son, in an age of uncertainties, as national symbols of optimism, stability and romance. Their first year of marriage also established roles for both parents that may ultimately prove more satisfying and rewarding than any other, that of husband and wife, father and mother.

As the Archbishop of Canterbury said in St Paul's Cathedral during their marriage service, 'Those who are married live happily ever after the wedding day if they persevere in the real adventure which is the royal task of creating each other and creating a more loving world . . . May the burdens we lay on them be matched by the love with which we support them in the years to come.'

Most of the photographs in this chapter were taken by Tim Graham including those on the Birthday stamps. The following, however, also supplied pictures for reproduction: Camera Press (Photos: Snowdon), pages 156, 158; Central Press, page 150 (left); courtesy of Crown Agents, page 157; The Press Association, page 160. The author and publishers would also like to thank Susie Elliott for her help with the astrological forecast on this page.

OVERLEAF: *The christening of Prince William took place in Buckingham Palace on 4 August 1982.*